MidKent College
LEARNING RESOURCE CENTRE

Medway Campus

Class No: _____ 822 _____

WEB

Return on or before the date last stamped below:

For renewals phone 01634 383044

PETER PANTO

Freely adapted from the book by J M Barrie

by Peter Webster from an idea by Finn Clark

WARNER/CHAPPELL PLAYS

LONDON

A Warner Music Group Company

PETER PANTO
First published in 1996
by Warner/Chappell Plays Ltd
129 Park Street, London W1Y 3FA

Copyright © 1994, 1996 by Peter Webster

The author asserts his moral right to be identified as the author of the work.

ISBN 0 85676 221 0

CAST

MR DARLING	
MRS DARLING	
WENDY	Their daughter
JOHN	Their elder son
MICHAEL	Their younger son
PETER PAN	
TINKERBELL	A fairy
CAPTAIN HOOK	A dastardly pirate
SMEE	His first mate
THE PIRATES	STARKEY
	JUKES
	COOKSON
	MULLINS
	CECCO
THE LOST BOYS	SLIGHTLY
	TOOTLES
	CURLY
	NIBS
	FIRST TWIN
	SECOND TWIN
NANA	A dog

CHORUS of pirates, forest spirits, animals, etc (as required by the director).

SCENES

ACT ONE

ACT TWO

ACT ONE

Scene One

Overture of songs used in the show. Some suggestions for suitable songs are made in the text, but directors are free to choose their own songs and to change their place in the action.

The whole cast is assembled. The curtains open to the first number, which should be slow and gentle on a magical/starry theme. (e.g. " The Second Star to the Right", "Do You Believe in Magic", etc.) The rear of the stage is in darkness — the rest of the stage is quite dark but is bathed in a dreamlike starry light. It would help if the cast could be cloaked and masked.

At the end of the number the stage empties quietly and the lights come up partially on an Edwardian style nursery set. This can be as elaborate as desired, or simply suggested by props rather than detailed construction/ painting. The only essentials are a door, a practical window large enough to climb through and a bed/mattress large enough for three.

After a few seconds a face appears at the window — it is PETER. *He quickly disappears — but soon peers in again when he sees it is safe. He pushes the window open slightly — at this moment* MRS DARLING *enters with* MICHAEL, *who is carrying a bear. She is carrying a lamp — the stage lighting goes up accordingly, but should still convey a type of lighting before electricity.* MRS DARLING *is a gentle, attractive woman dressed for an evening out.* MICHAEL *is the youngest of the three children, enthusiastic, gullible, sounding his' s' as 'th'. As soon as* PETER *sees her he drops out of sight.*

MRS DARLING	That's funny — I'm sure there was someone there at the window.
MICHAEL	Don't be thilly Mummy, how could there be unless they could fly, we're three floors up!
MRS DARLING	I know dear, of course you are right — but still I could have sworn there was someone there. Perhaps we shouldn't go out after all.
MICHAEL	We'll be alright — we are quite thafe with Nana around.
MRS DARLING	I suppose so. Now come on, time for bed!
	(JOHN *and* WENDY *enter.* JOHN *is a typical, worldly wise big brother to* MICHAEL, *but* WENDY *is the sensible, capable eldest child.)*
JOHN	Mother, Wendy is nagging me again — I do clean my teeth but I do it in my own good time.
WENDY	Yes, about once a week!

JOHN	You are a fibber!
WENDY	No I'm not!
JOHN	Yes you are!
WENDY	Not!
JOHN	Are!

MRS DARLING Children, children — do stop squabbling and get into bed. Your father will be ready in a minute and then we must go. Come along.

(There is much business here of getting comfortable and sorting out favourite soft toys, with a certain amount of pushing, shoving and generally establishing a space. MRS DARLING tucks them in, kisses each one and goes to stand at the foot of the bed.)

MRS DARLING We are going to dinner at your Aunt Agatha's. We shall not be late. While we are out Wendy is in charge — you must do as she says.

JOHN
MICHAEL } As usual!

MRS DARLING If you are worried at all, fetch Nana for company.

(NANA is heard barking offstage.)

MRS DARLING Why there she is now. She knows when we are talking about her.

(NANA enters and bounds across to the bed, causing chaos by licking each child in turn.)

WENDY
JOHN
MICHAEL } Nana, stop it!

MRS DARLING That's quite enough!

(The noise subsides. MR DARLING enters. He is a successful, middle-class man. He is wearing evening dress.)

MR DARLING What on earth's all this noise — I thought you were all in bed?

MRS DARLING They are dear, we were just saying good night.

MR DARLING Well hurry up or we shall be late. You know how Aunt Agatha hates it if the vichyssoise gets warm.

MRS DARLING	Don't fuss dear. Anyway, I'm really not sure we should leave them at all tonight. I am convinced that something odd has been happening.
MR DARLING	Odd! What sort of odd?
MRS DARLING	Well to begin with, I am sure I saw someone looking in at the window tonight. A boy I think. And tonight is not the first time — I have seen him before.
MR DARLING	Nonsense! How could there be someone outside the window?
MRS DARLING	I know it is nonsense. Nevertheless, I feel uneasy about leaving them.
JOHN	Oh, mother!
WENDY	We'll be fine.
MICHAEL	I'm not afraid.
MRS DARLING	He was trying to get in I tell you. A week ago I was sleeping by the fire and I suddenly felt a draught. I looked around and saw a boy trying to climb through the window — into the room.
MR DARLING	Oh really, dear!
MRS DARLING	I screamed and he leapt out. I sprang to the window and quickly closed it — but I was too late to catch him. The boy escaped, George. But his shadow caught on the catch.
WENDY	Oh, mother. How exciting — why didn't you keep the shadow?
MRS DARLING	I did, I rolled it up and hid it under the bed.
	(*She produces a shadow from underneath the bed and unrolls it.*)
MR DARLING	Talk about chasing shadows!
MRS DARLING	I think he returns for his shadow.
WENDY	You had better keep it safe then.
	(*The shadow is replaced.*)
MR DARLING	Oh, really! This is ridiculous — boys — shadows! Whatever next? Come along Mary — we shall be late. Good night children.
WENDY JOHN } MICHAEL	Goodnight, daddy.

MRS DARLING   Goodnight children. Sleep tight.

WENDY
JOHN   } Hope the bugs don't bite!
MICHAEL

MRS DARLING   Come along, Nana.

(MR *and* MRS DARLING *go with* NANA, *taking the light. The stage lights drop accordingly — all goes quiet for a few moments.* PETER *appears at the window — he starts to open it.* NANA *bounds in, barking madly.* PETER *immediately drops out of sight.*)

WENDY   (*sitting up*) Be quiet Nana! What's the matter with you? Go back to bed!

(NANA *'points' at the window and continues barking.* WENDY *gets up and checks all the corners of the room.*)

There's no one there — go away!

(NANA *goes quiet and slinks out. Once more there is peace — once more* PETER *appears.* NANA *repeats the performance.*)

WENDY   } Shut up, Nana!
JOHN

(NANA *rushes about madly and barks more wildly.*)

WENDY   Nana, be quiet!!

JOHN   Stop barking — there's nothing to bark at!

WENDY   Go away! Now!!

(NANA *ceases barking and slinks away again.*)

(*Once more there is silence —* PETER *reappears at the window and starts to climb through.* NANA *rushes in straight to the window and barks even more loudly.* WENDY, JOHN *and* MICHAEL *sit bolt upright in unison.*)

WENDY
JOHN   } Shut up, you horrible dog!
MICHAEL

(NANA *continues barking. The children jump out of bed and chase* NANA, *who constantly tries to reach the window, but is finally cornered.*)

WENDY   Bad dog! You are banished to your kennel!

(NANA *howls.*)

MICHAEL	Aah!

(*He encourages the audience.*)

AUDIENCE	Aah!

(*This can be prolonged according to reaction.*)

WENDY	It's no good Nana. To your kennel!

(NANA *whimpers — then goes quiet. The children take her out, and after a few moments they return and get back into bed.*)

JOHN	Thank goodness for that.
MICHAEL	Peath at last.
WENDY	Go to sleep.

(*Silence. Pale moonlight shines through the window.* PETER *appears once more at the window, opens it quietly and climbs in followed by* TINKERBELL, *who lands heavily.* TINKERBELL *is the antithesis of a traditional fairy, being noisy, self-opinionated and touchy. However she is devoted to* PETER. *She wears a rugby shirt, a neon pink tutu, striped tights, Doc Marten boots and bunches.*)

PETER	Sssh!
TINK	I am shushing. Gordon Bennett! Who turned out the lights?
PETER	I thought fairies were meant to be gentle and retiring!
TINK	I'm not that old! Anyway it's my day off. Look for your shadow!

(*They both tiptoe around the room, peering in all the corners — in a most exaggerated manner.* PETER *stops and bends down to look —* TINK *cannons into him.*)

PETER	}	(*turning into each other*) Sssh!
TINK		

(*More business in a similar vein can be added here if desired. Eventually* TINK *peers under the bed.*)

TINK	I think it's here!

(*She begins to tug at the shadow.* WENDY *stirs.*)

PETER	Be careful!

(TINK *tugs the shadow free and she falls over backwards.* WENDY *wakes, sees* TINK *and gives a small scream.* JOHN *and*

	MICHAEL *sleep on blissfully, accompanied by occasional grunts and snores.*)
TINK	Ooh er! Here's your shadow, let's run for it!
PETER	For once Tink, I agree!
	(*They both rush to the window — they try to climb through together.* TINK *being the most aggressive, makes most progress.*)
	Do hurry up!
	(*He gives her a helpful push and* TINK *disappears from view. There is a tremendous crash — then silence.*)
	Whoops! Sorry, Tink!
TINK	Sorry! I'll give you sorry!
PETER	I do hope she's all right.
WENDY	So do I. This is the third floor.
PETER	What's your name?
WENDY	Wendy Moira Angela Darling. What's yours?
PETER	(*finding it lamentably brief*) Peter Pan.
WENDY	Is that all?
PETER	(*biting his lip*) Yes.
WENDY	I am sorry.
PETER	It doesn't matter. Nice place you have here.
WENDY	Yes. Do you like that picture? (*Indicating a reproduction of a famous painting.*) It was handed down to us by my grandfather. Daddy says he was still on the ladder when the police arrived. Where do you live?
PETER	Past the second star to the right and straight on till morning.
WENDY	What a strange address.
PETER	No it isn't, everybody knows where it is.
WENDY	Well, what do they put on your letters?
PETER	I don't get any letters.
WENDY	Not even from your mother?
PETER	I don't have a mother.

WENDY	Peter, how awful!

(WENDY *tries to put her arms round him, but he draws back instinctively.*)

WENDY	Is that why you came into my bedroom?
PETER	Certainly not! I came to reclaim my shadow. I lost it — here.
WENDY	Has it come off? How awful! It must be sewn on.
PETER	What does sewn mean?
WENDY	You are dreadfully ignorant.
PETER	No I'm not.
WENDY	Yes you are!
PETER	No I'm not! (*Etc.*)
WENDY	Come here and sit by me, I will sew it on for you. I dare say it might hurt a little.
PETER	I don't mind, I never cry.
WENDY	What never?
PETER	Well, hardly ever.

(WENDY *fetches thimble, needle and thread from a work basket and sews on the shadow. When she has finished,* PETER *tests his shadow. He dances round the room, generally showing off and practising the crowing that will come in useful at a later point in the play.*)

PETER	It's done! Wendy look aren't I clever, I'm back to normal!
WENDY	You conceited beast! Of course, I did nothing!

(*Opportunity for a song on the subject of vanity — such as "You're so vain". This can be done as a solo for* WENDY *or as a duet.*)

PETER	Well yes, I suppose you did help a little.

(WENDY *gets into bed and pulls the sheet over her face.* PETER *goes to her.*)

PETER	Wendy, I'm sorry. I can't help crowing when I'm pleased with myself. Wendy, one girl is worth a dozen boys.
WENDY	You really think so, Peter?
PETER	Yes, I do.

WENDY   I think that's perfectly sweet of you and I shall get up again.

(*They sit together on the bed.*)

WENDY   I shall give you a kiss as a reward for being brave.

PETER   Thank you.

(*He holds out his hand.*)

WENDY   Don't you know what a kiss is?

PETER   I shall know when you give it to me.

(WENDY *dithers, clearly thrown by this display of unworldly innocence — she finally gives him her thimble.*)

PETER   Now I shall give you a kiss.

WENDY   If you please.

(*He pulls a button from his clothes and gives it to her.*)

WENDY   Well that's something to treasure! Very precious! What a man of the world you are. (*She smiles broadly.*) I will wear it on this chain around my neck. (*She threads the button on her chain while she talks.*) Peter, how old are you?

PETER   I don't know, Wendy. I ran away the day I was born.

WENDY   Ran away? Why?

PETER   I heard mother and father talking of what I was going to be when I became a man. I never want to grow up. I don't want to live in the real world.

WENDY   (*to audience*) He should become a judge.

PETER   I want to remain a boy and have fun. So I ran away to live in Never Land with the fairies and lost boys.

WENDY   You know fairies, Peter? Real ones?

PETER   (*surprised that this is a novelty*) Yes, but they are nearly all dead now. You see Wendy, when the first baby laughed for the first time, the laugh broke into a thousand pieces and that was the beginning of the fairies. Now when a new baby is born, its first laugh becomes a fairy. So there should be one fairy for every boy or girl.

WENDY   Should be? Isn't there?

PETER   Oh no. Children know such a lot now. Soon they don't believe in fairies and every time a child says "I don't believe in fairies", a fairy somewhere falls down dead.

WENDY	Poor things. How awful.
PETER	Speaking of awful things, that reminds me. Tink! I can't think where she has got to. Tinkerbell, where are you?
WENDY	Is she the one you pushed out of the window?
PETER	Uh oh! I forgot.
WENDY	I think we had better look for her.
	(*The two go to the window, and peer through.*)
PETER	Tink! Are you all right?
TINK	(*after an ominous silence*) Not bad, apart from the agonizing pain.
WENDY	We need a rope. Ah, I know!
	(WENDY *pulls a sheet from the bed and throws the end through the window. She and* PETER *then pull it in —* TINK *appears at the end. She is somewhat dishevelled.*)
TINK	About time too! For all you cared, I could have been squashed flat as a pancake while you chatted up your fancy bit!
WENDY	(*taking an instant dislike to* TINK) I'm sorry, did you say you were a fairy?
TINK	Yes. And a strikingly beautiful one, too.
WENDY	Does that mean that you are in disguise? You are only pretending to be an old bag?
TINK	Slanderer! I have everything a man could desire.
WENDY	A deep voice, a luxuriant moustache, a hairy chest.
TINK	That girl should go far. As far as possible!
WENDY	Tinkerbell, you lack an indefinable something.
TINK	What?
WENDY	Charm!
TINK	What cheek! Always remember that I am a lady.
WENDY	Don't worry, your secret is safe with me.
TINK	Be careful what you say to me, I have friends in high places.
WENDY	You mean swinging from trees in the jungle?
TINK	Well, I never did!

WENDY   I'm not surprised with a face like yours!

PETER   Ladies, ladies, please!

         (TINK *flounces over to the window*.)

WENDY   Humph! Peter, who are the lost boys you mentioned?

PETER   Oh, them! They are the children who fall out of their prams
         while their mothers are looking the other way. If they are not
         found and claimed in seven days, they go to Never Land. I'm
         their chief.

WENDY   Are you? How exciting!

PETER   Yes, but we are rather lonely — we have no female
         companionship. Girls are much too clever to fall out of their
         prams.

WENDY   I think it is perfectly lovely the way you talk about girls. John
         there just despises us.

PETER   Oh, does he? (PETER *looks at* JOHN, *then goes to him and tips
         him out of bed*.)

WENDY   Peter, you wicked thing! You're not chief here.

         (WENDY *goes to* JOHN, *who is still snoring happily*.)

PETER   Does he do that for a living?

WENDY   No, it's just a talent he has. (*Looking hard at* TINK.) Peter, you
         may give me a kiss.

PETER   I thought you would want it back. (*He offers her the thimble*.)

WENDY   Oh, dear. I didn't mean a kiss, Peter. I meant a thimble.

PETER   What's a thimble?

WENDY   It's one of these. (*She kisses him on the cheek.* PETER *feels his
         cheek, somewhat nonplussed. He is now a very confused
         young man*.)

PETER   Is that a thimble?

WENDY   Yes. Do you want to give me a thimble?

TINK   Oh, no he doesn't!

WENDY   Oh, yes he does! (*Repeated as desired*.)

PETER   Mind your manners Tink. I have never known you so rude! If I
         want to thimble Wendy, I'll thimble her.

WENDY   (*melting*) Do you want to, Peter?

PETER	Er . . . no. I don't think so just at the moment, thank you.
	(*The idea of thimbling scares him much more than* CAPTAIN HOOK *ever will.*)
WENDY	Why not?
PETER	Well. It's just that . . .
WENDY	Never mind. Why did you first come to our window?
PETER	To hear stories. None of us know any stories.
WENDY	How depressing! A deprived childhood if ever I saw one.
PETER	Your mother was telling you such a lovely story.
WENDY	Which story was it?
TINK	The one about the hedgehog and the steamroller.
PETER	Be quiet, Tink! It was the one about the prince who couldn't find the lady with the glass slipper.
WENDY	That was Cinderella! They got married and lived happy ever after.
TINK	Yuk, yuk, yuk! I feel sick!
PETER	Married? (*Something tells him he should be worried. He makes for the window.*)
WENDY	Where are you going?
PETER	Er . . . to tell the others about Cinderella.
WENDY	Don't go, Peter. I know lots of stories. Stories I could tell to you and the lost boys.
PETER	(*suddenly all fear forgotten, an idea*) Come with me! Come and see Never Land. We'll fly!
WENDY	Fly? Can you fly?
PETER	Of course! Can't you? Come with me Wendy!
TINK	I think it's a rotten idea!
PETER WENDY }	Oh, no it isn't!
TINK	Oh, yes it is! (*Repeat as desired.*)
WENDY	Oh dear! I don't think I should — think of mother and father. Besides I can't fly.

PETER	I'll teach you. Let me show you all the wonders of my land. It's not far — if you use your imagination.
WENDY	Could John and Michael come too?
PETER	I suppose so — if they must.
WENDY	(*shaking* JOHN *and* MICHAEL *hard*) John! Michael! Wake up! Peter is going to teach us to fly.
JOHN	(*sleepily*) Peter? Who's Peter?
WENDY	(*realising they do not know* PETER) This boy.
MICHAEL	(*seeing* TINK) Whoth that?
TINK	I'm the fairy Tinkerbell.
MICHAEL	You're rather big for a fairy.
TINK	I'm not big! Just big boned. It's a sign of sensitivity.
WENDY	I'd be sensitive about it too.
JOHN	Wendy, did you say fly?
WENDY	Of course, Peter can do anything.
PETER	Absolutely! I once made an elephant fly.
JOHN	An elephant? You mean Tinkerbell?
PETER	(*fearing instant reprisals*) No, no! I mean a real elephant.
	(*Cue for a song — "When I See an Elephant Fly", sung by* PETER *with the others joining in, with appropriate actions.*)
MICHAEL	Thath fine for elephants but how do we fly?
PETER	That's easy. You simply need fairy dust. Tink!
TINK	Must I ? This stuff is expensive you know.
PETER	Yes you must, otherwise this story won't get anywhere. She must, mustn't she audience?
TINK	Oh no, I mustn't!
AUDIENCE	Oh yes you must! (*Repeat as desired.*)
PETER	That's enough Tink. Get on with it!
	(TINK *scatters a tiny amount of dust over them.*)
PETER	Tink! More!
	(TINK *scatters slightly more.*)
	Tink, I shan't tell you again!

TINK	Have it you're own way. (*She deluges them in dust. Everyone coughs and splutters.*)
JOHN	Is that it?
MICHAEL	(*jumping up and down*) It'h not working!
TINK	You're trying too hard. It will work once you jump out of the window.
JOHN	But this is the third floor!
PETER	All the better. Gives you more time to get the hang of it.
WENDY	If I wanted never to grow up, I'd jump out of a third floor window, too.
PETER	Come on, Wendy. You trust me don't you?
WENDY	Do I ? Yes, of course I do.
	(PETER *holds out his hand.* WENDY *takes it — they go to the window.* TINK *is waiting there impatiently.*)
JOHN	You're not going with him?
WENDY	I . . . I . . . yes!
JOHN	But it may be dangerous. If father could see you now, he'd have a fit.
PETER	Of course, it's dangerous on the island. There are pirates and indians and wild animals . . .
MICHAEL	Piwathes! Let'th get them, John!
	(MICHAEL *pulls* JOHN *towards the window, and holds* WENDY'S *hand.*)
JOHN	I really don't think . . .
WENDY	Come on, slowcoach!
	(*Everyone steps through the window in turn. Fading shouts of "I can fly", etc. The lights go down, to a repeat of the music of the opening song which suddenly changes into a sinister introduction for* CAPTAIN HOOK.)

Scene Two

CAPTAIN HOOK *enters in front of half tabs, lit by a follow spot. He wears the traditional restoration style clothes, complete with long wig. He is thoroughly evil and enjoys being so — he is also very refined in many ways. An iron claw replaces one of his hands — this must look convincing.*

| HOOK | More, more! That's my kind of music — not that soppy rubbish you have been suffering so far! |
| AUDIENCE | Boo! Hiss! |

(HOOK *should encourage this, taking a bow and generally revelling in his notoriety.*)

HOOK	Silence, you nauseating softy landlubbers! You are in the august presence of Captain Jas Hook of the good ship the Jolly Roger. I'm the evilest, most vicious, most sadistic pirate on the seven seas — I am also the handsomest and most desirable. I am so bad I was thrown out of the Mafia for unnecessary cruelty. I'm a consultant to the Spanish Inquisition! I will tell you now that I'm going to do away with Peter Pan and enslave his friends. I am also going to make your lives a living hell!
AUDIENCE	Boo. Hiss!
HOOK	Shut up, I said! You haven't brought any children with you, have you? I hate children and I hate Peter Pan most of all. He pollutes my island with laughter and songs, he feeds the crocodile, he encourages the mermaids to work on Timotei and Bounty ads — and doesn't take any fees. He is not interested in power or money — in short he's the sort of boy who makes me think the Pied Piper wasn't such a bad fellow after all. His friends are no better — they are all horrors. The only time I like children is when I go to the playground and watch them screaming and jumping up and down — I've wired the swings to the mains! Mind you, I have my sensitive side too — I like to sing. In fact I'm going to sing now — you would like to hear me sing wouldn't you?
AUDIENCE	No!
HOOK	Oh, yes you would!
AUDIENCE	Oh, no we wouldn't!
HOOK	Tough! This song is for all you lovely ladies out there. To Davy Jones with it — it's for all you ugly ones, too.

(*Song. Something nasty is called for here, such as Tom Lehrer's "Poisoning Pigeons in the Park".*)

| HOOK | (*as the song ends*) Now where are my jolly dogs? Well met, my bullies! |

(*Enter the* PIRATES — *they are traditionally rough and tough, all except* SMEE *who is not sure he is cut out to be a pirate. He might have preferred to be an accountant. He tries to use pirate speak when he remembers.* HOOK *would rather he did, in order to set an example.*)

PIRATES	(*in unison all except* SMEE, *in very gruff voices*) YO HO, YO HO, THE PIRATE LIFE THE FLAG OF SKULL AND BONES. A MERRY HOUR, A HEMPEN ROPE AND HEY FOR DAVY JONES!
SMEE	(*lightly*) Hi, sorry we're late.
HOOK	(*menacingly*) Hi! Are you sure you wouldn't like to try that again and this time do it properly!
SMEE	Sorry Captain. (*In true piratey manner.*) Ahahahaharrrr, Cap'n. Aharah, hah!
HOOK	That's better! Why are you late?
SMEE	We came by the scenic route and got carried away by the beauty of the sunset.
HOOK	Bah! What have I done to be landed with an aesthetic pirate? Have you found those boys yet, Smee?
SMEE	Not a sausage yet, chief.
HOOK	Smee!
	(HOOK *glowers.* SMEE *drops back into yo-ho-ho mode and wriggles guiltily.*)
SMEE	Sorry, Cap'n. But they do say Peter Pan be returning to the Never Land, ahar. Ahahahahrrrr. We'll get rid of him this time, Cap'n, by fair means or foul. We must devise a cunning plan.
HOOK	Preferably something foul — much more fun. Pan! 'Twas he that cut off my hand.
SMEE	But that hook's right useful innit, Cap'n. 'Tis worth a score of hands for combing hair and other homely uses. See, I got it right then didn't I?
HOOK	If I were a mother Smee, I would pray for my children to be so equipped. But I had no choice, did I Smee? Oh, no. 'Twas Pan that cut off my hand and flung it to the crocodile.
SMEE	Yeah, I have noticed that you are scared witless of crocs.
HOOK	Smee! I shall not tell you again. Confine yourself to our fine pirate's banter. However, I digress. I am not scared of crocodiles in general, but of that crocodile in particular. The brute liked the taste of me so much that he has pursued me ever since in the hope of consuming the rest of me.

SMEE   It's a sort of compliment I suppose.

HOOK   I have no need of such compliments. That crocodile would
                have had me by now, but luckily he swallowed my watch
                along with my hand. (*Aside, to the audience.*) Those of you
                still awake may have noticed a minor anachronism — pray
                don't let it trouble you, this is after all a story about time. (*To*
                SMEE.) Before he can reach me I hear the ticking inside him
                and bolt.

SMEE   Blimey, sounds like an advertising agency — Ticking Inside
                Him And Bolt.

                (HOOK *cuffs his ear.*)

                Ow, that hurt! (*Rubbing his ear and shaking his finger at*
                HOOK, *both at the same time.*) You'd better hope your watch
                doesn't run down then, otherwise you'll be in deep . . .

HOOK   Smee, take care!

SMEE   Trouble. Oh, um — t'would be an unfortunate circumstance,
                Cap'n. Yo-ho-ho. Pieces of eight and tankards of rum!

HOOK   The watch won't run down — it's electric.

SMEE   Electric? How does it go?

HOOK   Well, Smee the principle of electricity is as follows. Now
                concentrate if you please.

SMEE   No Cap'n, how does it sound?

HOOK   Sound? Well it goes sort of tic-toc.

                (*A loud ticking is heard from offstage.*)

HOOK   Rather like that — very similar.

SMEE   Exactly like that?

HOOK   Exactly. Capering cutlasses! It's him — the crocodile! Run
                Smee, run, but let me get a head start!

                (*The* PIRATES *scatter offstage. Enter the* CROCODILE *searching
                for a tasty meal. He stops, snaps his teeth at the audience
                then exits in pursuit. The ticking stops. The half tabs open to
                Scene Three.*)

                                Scene Three

*Never Land. This can be represented by a fantastical, larger-than-life forest
painted in cartoon-like colours — this could also be somewhat nightmarish as
the Never Land is not all sweetness and light, but has its share of dangers.
Enter the* LOST BOYS *at something of a loss without their leader —* SECOND

TWIN *is missing. They are dressed in tattered shorts and shirts, adorned with scraps of fur and feathers and wearing a crude attempt at warpaint. Their characters can reflect the people who play them.*

NIBS	What are we going to do?
CURLY	I don't know. Why ask me?
TOOTLES	Because you think you're so clever.
SLIGHTLY	Don't start all that again.
NIBS	Who's starting?
FIRST TWIN	You are. As always.
NIBS	What do you mean by that?
TOOTLES	Well, you are an old bossy boots.
CURLY	You can talk!
TOOTLES	Say that again!
CURLY	Bossy boots!
TOOTLES	Right, you asked for it!

(TOOTLES *thumps* CURLY, *who retaliates but only succeeds in hitting* FIRST TWIN, *who falls over* NIBS. *There is pandemonium as a free-for-all ensues. They are all totally ineffective and only succeed in wasting a great deal of energy. Realising this, they gradually extricate themselves from the resulting heap of bodies.*)

NIBS   This is getting us nowhere. I do wish Peter would come back, he would know what to do. Now Hook has captured Second Twin, we must make a plan to get him back — but I'm not good at making plans. The ideas are good, but they get mixed up in the telling.

TOOTLES   I always worry about those pirates when Peter is not here to keep them in check. Losing Second Twin gives us good reason to worry.

SLIGHTLY   They don't worry me! Nothing worries me, but I do wish Peter would come back and tell us about Cinderella.

TOOTLES   I am awfully anxious about Cinderella. You see, I think she was like my mother.

CURLY   You mean covered with ash and wearing unsuitable shoes?

FIRST TWIN   I remember my mother was one of twins.

NIBS   How could you tell them apart?

FIRST TWIN   Her brother had a beard.

CURLY   My mother couldn't leave her bed.

TOOTLES   Why not?

CURLY   Father had sewn her into the mattress.

NIBS   My heavens! That's matricide.

SLIGHTLY   My mother was fonder of me than your mothers were of you.

ALL   Oh, no she wasn't!

SLIGHTLY   Oh, yes she was! Peter had to make up names for you lot, but my mother put my name on my vest — "Slightly Soiled", that's my name.

              (TINK *enters at high speed.*)

TINK   Howdy, Boys!

CURLY   Hello Tink, is Peter back yet?

TINK   No, but I have a message for you from him. There's a big white bird flying this way. He wants you to shoot it.

FIRST TWIN   Where is it?

TINK   Up there, coming this way.

              (TINK *points in the air, offstage from whence she came.*)

TOOTLES   I see it. Isn't it lovely. What's it called?

TINK   A Wendy.

SLIGHTLY   (*instantly*) I remember now, there are birds called Wendies.

TINK   Stop gabbing! Quick, shoot it before Peter gets here!

NIBS   Before Peter gets here?

TINK   Er . . . so he won't have to do it himself.

NIBS   I don't think we should shoot the Wendy. It's neither environmentally friendly or politically correct. Let's ask the audience. Do you think we should shoot the Wendy?

AUDIENCE   No!

TINK   Oh, yes they should!

AUDIENCE   Oh, no they shouldn't!

(*Repeated according to reaction, with appropriate encouragement from* TINK *and the* BOYS. TINK *dashes offstage and returns with a bow and arrow, giving them to* TOOTLES.)

TINK   But Peter wishes it — so get on with it!

TOOTLES   Oh, alright.

(TOOTLES *takes careful aim and shoots into the wings. There is a short silence then a distant scream from* WENDY.)

TOOTLES   I hit the Wendy! What a shot! Peter will be so pleased. Let's go and retrieve it.

(*The* BOYS *race off leaving* TINK *whistling to herself and examining her fingernails. They return shortly carrying* WENDY *with her hands clasped across her chest, like Ophelia. They put her down and crowd round.*)

FIRST TWIN   This is no bird. I have a bad feeling about this.

CURLY   I think it must be a lady.

NIBS   And Tootles has killed her.

SLIGHTLY   And Peter was bringing her to us.

CURLY   To take care of us?

ALL   Oh, Tootles. What have you done?

TOOTLES   I didn't want to do it, but Tink made me. I was only carrying out orders. I always wanted a mother, but when she really came I shot her.

(TOOTLES *drops to his knees, drawing his knife as if to end it all. There is a moment of horrified silence.*)

TOOTLES   Friends, goodbye!

ALL   (*except* TINK) Don't do it!

TOOTLES   I must. Peter will never forgive me for this — goodbye!

(*He raises his knife — to the strains of a violin. At this moment* PETER *is heard calling offstage.*)

ALL   Peter!

(*Everybody surrounds* WENDY *as* PETER *enters.*)

PETER   Greetings boys!

(*There is dead silence.*)

PETER   What's the matter? Aren't you pleased to see me?

SLIGHTLY	Oh, yes of course. It's just that we don't know what to do. You see we've just had a bit of an accident.
CURLY	(*stamping on* SLIGHTLY's *foot*) Er, yes. We have lost Second Twin.
NIBS	Yes, Hook's got him.
FIRST TWIN	They ambushed us. We were overwhelmed.
SLIGHTLY	There were hundreds of them.
CURLY	Well several, anyway.
NIBS	And we all decided discretion was the better part of valour.
SLIGHTLY	Only Second Twin didn't decide fast enough and they caught him.
PETER	Oh, is that all? I thought something dreadful had happened by the looks on your faces. Don't worry. I know how to deal with Hook — we'll have him back in no time. But first things first. Great news — I have brought a mother for us all at last.

(*Again there is silence, with much staring into the air or examining of nails.*)

PETER	She flew this way. Did you not see her?
FIRST TWIN	(*very quietly*) Er, yes we did as a matter of fact.
PETER	What did you say? I can't hear you.
FIRST TWIN	I said " yes we did ".
SLIGHTLY NIBS } CURLY	Keep it hid!
TOOTLES	(*stepping forward*) It's no good. Peter, I will show you where she is.
SLIGHTLY NIBS } CURLY FIRST TWIN	(*shaking their heads in unison*) No, no. Bad move!
TOOTLES	I am a gentleman — I must.
SLIGHTLY NIBS } CURLY FIRST TWIN	Gentleman? Wally more like!

TOOTLES	Stand back all, let Peter see.

(*The human fence dissolves, revealing* WENDY *to* PETER'S *horrified gaze.*)

PETER	Wendy! Wendy? What's wrong?
CURLY	At the risk of stating the obvious, she's got an arrow in her chest.

(PETER *gently removes the arrow and holds it up.*)

PETER	Whose arrow? Come on, whose is it?

(*Everybody avoids looking at* TOOTLES, *who steps honourably forward.*)

TOOTLES	It's mine, Peter.
PETER	Then you too must die. It's the law — an eye for a nose and all that.

(PETER *slowly approaches* TOOTLES, *who drops to his knees, baring his chest.* PETER *raises the arrow to strike.* WENDY *groans —* PETER *drops the arrow and goes to her.*)

PETER	She lives!
SLIGHTLY	The Wendy lady lives!

(PETER *holds up a button attached to the chain around her neck.*)

PETER	See, the arrow struck against this. It is the kiss I gave her — it has saved her life.
CURLY	Fancy that! What a happy circumstance! Just as well, otherwise we'd have no story.
SLIGHTLY	I remember kisses — let me see it. (*He looks.*) Yes, that is a kiss.
PETER	We shall need a doctor. Slightly, fetch one!
SLIGHTLY	Where am I going to find a doctor in a hurry round here? This isn't Casualty you know! (*He goes.*)
WENDY	Where — where am I?
PETER	Don't worry Wendy, you will be alright. Help is on the way.

(SLIGHTLY *returns with* TINKERBELL. *She wears a stethoscope and carries a saw, pliers, etc, in a bag.*)

TINK   Yes, my little man?

PETER   Doctor, this lady is very ill. (*Indicating* WENDY.)

TINK   Oh, it's her. Obviously no hope — a real no-hoper.

WENDY   (*not at all reassured*) You're a doctor?

TINK   You'd better believe it. Just one of my many talents. I used to have a practice — I never quite got it right. Still you'll make a good guinea pig. Are you paying, or shall I hurt you?

PETER   What's wrong with her?

TINK   She's too fat.

WENDY   I want a second opinion.

TINK   You're ugly too.

PETER   Tink, behave! Can you cure her?

TINK   Of course. Just watch this.
            Doctor Tink with just some passes
            Cures the ills of all the classes.
            But for this treatment, please go private.
            Then there's a chance you might survive it.

            (TINK *makes some magic passes over* WENDY. WENDY *immediately relapses.*)

PETER   Nice one Tink. I suggest you try again, and this time add some fairy dust into the equation.

TINK   There you go again. Anyone would think this stuff was easy to come by — it's harder to find than water in Yorkshire. But I'll try once more, just for you.

            Once again I work my magic
            The outcome shouldn't be too tragic.
            I'll try sheer luck and fairy dust,
            If one don't work the other must!

            (TINK *makes more magic passes and sprinkles fairy dust over* WENDY. WENDY *slowly sits up and sneezes loudly.*)

PETER	How is she?
TINK	My treatment has cured her, just as I promised.
WENDY	I'm alright now, no thanks to Dr Frankenstein there.
PETER	Thank goodness. (*Suddenly and slowly.*) But *why* Tootles, why did you shoot Wendy?
TOOTLES	Er . . . 'cos . . . well . . . er. Tink said you wanted us to.
PETER	Tink. What have you done?
TINK	Tootles, you are a sneaking ratbag!
PETER	You told them to shoot Wendy? I am your friend no more.
TINK	I did it for you! I am your own personal, inseparable fairy.
PETER	You have done something horrible! I never want to see you again, never, ever, ever! Don't even set foot on this island for a million years!
TINK	Something tells me you're annoyed.
	(TINK *is deeply upset. She sniffles and starts to go, hands behind her, dragging her feet.*)
LOST BOYS	Aaaah!
	(TINK *encourages this from the boys and the audience.*)
AUDIENCE	Aaaah!
PETER	It's no good trying that one. My mind is made up. I am as stone — adamant, inflexible, immoveable.
TINK	Oh, you mean thick as a brick! Can I come back tomorrow?
PETER	Yes, alright.
	(TINK *exits.* WENDY *gets up and goes to* PETER.)
WENDY	Peter, is this the Never Land?
PETER	It is.
FIRST TWIN	And we are now all your children.
WENDY	What, all of you?

SLIGHTLY	Wendy lady, be our mother.
WENDY	Well, of course all this is very flattering, but I'm not really qualified to be your mother, I have no experience.
NIBS	We don't care, we just want a role model — on account we're deprived.
WENDY	More like depraved. Very well, you have twisted my arm — I will do my best.

(*Everyone cheers and capers about in a most unseemly manner.*)

WENDY	Quiet! I can see we are going to have to start with manners.
CURLY	Why? You seem quite polite to me.
WENDY	Not mine. Yours!

(JOHN *and* MICHAEL *enter, bewildered and very tired.*)

WENDY	John, Michael! Safe and sound at last!
JOHN	Then it's true, we did fly here. Wendy, where are we?
WENDY	The Never Land.
JOHN } MICHAEL	The Never Land? We've never heard of it!
FIRST TWIN	That's why it's called the Never Land.
SLIGHTLY	Yes, you may wonder. Actually, it's a creation of the human mind. We all need to believe it exists — or something like it.
NIBS	It's like dreaming.
WENDY	You mean if we wake up it will all disappear.
JOHN	Don't worry — they are all talking rubbish. This is all quite implausible.
CURLY	He's quite right. Actually, this is a parallel universe, connected to the real one by a time warp.
JOHN	Ah, I can believe that.

(*There is universal amazement.*)

SLIGHTLY   You do? You mean you do!

(*Everyone freezes except* CURLY.)

CURLY   (*to the audience*) At this point, audience, you must suspend
               belief even more — if that's possible.

(*A sign saying "Suspend Belief Now" is carried across the
stage.*)

LOST BOYS   A time warp it is!

(*This is an obvious cue for a song — "The Time Warp", from
the Rocky Horror Show. This could be a real show stopper,
but be wary of over enthusiastic gestures! As many chorus
members as desired could join in. At the end of the song the
chorus leave.*)

WENDY   Well boys, you've certainly had your fun and rather too much
               excitement for one day. We'd better go home now. I'm sure
               it's way past bedtime.

PETER   Home? What's a home?

WENDY   Well, it's a . . .

JOHN   It's a place to live. A house.

PETER   Do you want a house here?

WENDY   Definitely. I am used to certain standards.

PETER   Very well. Boys, build Wendy a house.

CURLY   What is a house exactly?

MICHAEL   Father says it's something you spend your life paying for,
               needs constant cleaning and is always in need of repair.

CURLY   And she still wants one?

PETER   Yes, so get on with it — let's see some effort.

(NIBS *falls to the ground in apparent agony.*)

NIBS   Aaaah! I've broken my leg! Oh, the pain! I shan't be able to do
               any work.

TOOTLES	Then why are you clutching your arm?
NIBS	I've a broken leg bone in my arm.
PETER	Nibs, if you don't help, I will personally feed you to the crocodile — piece by piece.

(NIBS *miraculously recovers*.)

FIRST TWIN	Nice try Nibs. That fall was about as convincing as an Italian centre forward.
NIBS	It was the least I could do.
SLIGHTLY	A quantity he specialises in.
NIBS	Are you going to help too, Peter?
PETER	Gosh, is that the time? (*Consulting the hairs on his wrist.*) We'll have to hurry if you want to see the mermaids Wendy, and we need to make plans to rescue Second Twin.
WENDY	When did I ever ask to see any mermaids, or to rescue anyone? (PETER *claps his hand over her mouth.*)
PETER	Ssssh! Bye, bye boys.

(PETER *and* WENDY *exit.*)

JOHN	Well, what do we do now?
SLIGHTLY	I don't know. What do you want to do?
JOHN	I don't know.
CURLY	For heavens sake! We'd better discuss it.

(*They all go into a huddle like American footballers. Rhubarb, rhubarb, etc.* TINK *enters.*)

TINK	Hello boys. Peter gone?
FIRST TWIN	Tink, what are you doing here?
TINK	I don't like leaving you lot, you'll only get into trouble. Anyway, what are you doing?
NIBS	We're building a house.
TINK	Oh, I know all about that. I'll show you what to do.

NIBS	What do we do first?
TINK	Get building materials of course! Anything you can lay your hands on.

(The boys start rushing around in search of suitable materials. This should look chaotic, but must in fact be carefully choreographed with much ducking, weaving and near misses. The boys bring on an assortment of tables, chairs, boards, etc, which appear totally unrelated but when put into place all fit together. Part of the front wall must be paper covered and the whole thing must be collapsible. When assembled the house must be behind the line of the half tabs. TINK takes a chair and sits in order to supervise events.)

TINK	Enough! Stop! That will do. Now, you've got your materials make a house shape.
CURLY	How do we do that?
TINK	Just sort of assemble it. Try to produce a featureless, monolithic box and stick a sign on it "architect designed". If that fails you can always get a grant from the Arts Council by calling it sculpture. We'll have this house built before you can say "Jack Robinson".
FIRST TWIN	But don't say it for about seven hours.
TINK	What are you waiting for? Go, go, go!

(The boys fit their assorted collection together at high speed. This again must not look rehearsed, but is! The dialogue continues. CURLY decides to read a paper he has found.)

TINK	Be careful of that wood, it doesn't grow on trees you know! Curly, what are you doing?
CURLY	Reading.
TINK	Give me that! What were you reading about anyway?
CURLY	The effect of nationalistic tendencies on the international political arena.
TINK	Surely not! (TINK *gets up to look.*)
CURLY	Yes, that piece on page three. And don't call me Shirley.

TINK	Well, don't let me catch you again. You are supposed to be working.
	(TINK *returns to her chair, just as* FIRST TWIN *takes it for the house. The inevitable happens.*)
	Aaaah! (*As she falls she clutches at* TOOTLES, *who falls on top of her.*)
TOOTLES	Why Tink, I didn't know you cared!
TINK	Who took my chair? Own up! Who took my chair?
FIRST TWIN	I thought you could stand on your own two feet.
	(FIRST TWIN *picks up a long board left over. He wanders about looking for somewhere to put it, making everyone duck.*)
TINK	I'm alright. I can take it, I'm a modern woman.
MICHAEL	Are you emanthipated then?
TINK	Oh, definitely.
TOOTLES	You want to try Eno's then.
CURLY	We've paid for these jokes, audience, and we are going to use them.
TINK	(*considering the house*) Not bad, not bad. Straight out of the Blue Peter do it yourself manual. We'll come to the inside next. Remember the curtains can be drawn, but the furniture must be real.
	(FIRST TWIN *hits* TINK *with his plank, which the audience should have been anticipating for some time now. She goes clean through the front wall.*)
FIRST TWIN	Whoops! Sorry! Well at least the ground broke your fall. Let me help you up.
TINK	No. No! Keep him away from me! (*She crawls away.*)
	(FIRST TWIN *moves away, but only succeeds in hitting her backside in retreat. He tries to help her up, but she hits her head on part of the house.*)
TINK	Aaaooooww!
FIRST TWIN	Sorry. Did that hurt?

(TINK *says nothing, but goes purposefully off stage. She returns with a tray bearing custard pies*.)

TINK   Twin, come here!

FIRST TWIN   Why?

TINK   I've got a present for you.

FIRST TWIN   It's not a custard pie, is it?

TINK   No, no, of course not!

FIRST TWIN   Is it audience?

AUDIENCE   Yes!

TINK   Oh, no it's not!

FIRST TWIN   Oh, yes it is! (*Etc.*)

TINK   Well, yes perhaps it is.

FIRST TWIN   You were going to hit me!

TINK   (*to audience*) Would I do a thing like that?

AUDIENCE   Yes!

TINK   Spoilsports! You've been here before.

FIRST TWIN   I shall defend myself. (*He takes a custard pie.*)

JOHN   A duel?

FIRST TWIN   A duel!

                (TINK *and* FIRST TWIN *stand back to back. Drum roll.*)

TINK   Ten paces. Count them out!

                (SLIGHTLY *counts.* FIRST TWIN *and* TINK *take a pace on each count.*)

SLIGHTLY   One, two, three, four, er — thumb.

MICHAEL   Five, thix, theven.

                (TINK *turns and sneaks up on* FIRST TWIN.)

MICHAEL	Eight!
AUDIENCE	She's behind you!
FIRST TWIN	What's that? I can't hear.
MICHAEL	Nine!
AUDIENCE	She's behind you!
FIRST TWIN	What's that again audience, I can't hear?
MICHAEL	Ten. Geronimo!

(TINK *tries to hit* FIRST TWIN. *He ducks and hits* TINK *in the face with his pie instead.*)

FIRST TWIN	I bet you thought I was going to get splatted, didn't you audience?

(*He swaggers around lost in self adulation, trips and falls face down on the tray of pies.*)

JOHN	Well I'm sure this is all great fun, but we can't waste time like this getting nowhere. People will think we are (local) town councillors.
TINK	(*wiping her face*) He's right. The house needs decorating. I'm going to cast a spell.

(*Everyone runs for cover.*)

TINK	Oh, come on! I'm a fairy, I can do magic. I'm not that bad.
TOOTLES	Then why does nothing you do ever work?
TINK	How dare you, I'm the finest magician in Never Land!
ALL	You're the only magician in Never Land!
TINK	I'm one in a thousand!
SLIGHTLY	That's also the definition of an epidemic.
TINK	You can't stop me! Abracadabra, zipadeedoo!
NIBS	We must stop her. We are all in the gravest danger!
TINK	Don't be so silly! Abracadabra, abracadabra!

(TINK *gestures grandly. Nothing happens for a few moments — then there is a flash, an explosion and the house falls down.*)

TINK   (*surveying the ruins*) Whoops!

                (*The curtains close.*)

                                Scene Four

Initially in front of half tabs. PETER *and* WENDY *enter.*

WENDY   I think that was really rotten of you to make up that excuse about going to see mermaids, just to get out of doing some work! And you're supposed to set an example.

PETER   I'm sorry, but I did it for the best of reasons — to get you to myself for a bit. You had me really worried   I thought you would die.

WENDY   In that case I forgive you. But you needn't worry — I'm fine. I think it's good to be with you too.

                (*Cue for a song, such as Leo Sayer's "When I need you". During the song, the debris of the house are cleared away and the scene set to represent the shore of the Mermaids Lagoon. During the song* TINK *tries to sweep round them with a large broom, thus totally destroying any feeling of romance.* PETER *tries unavailingly to shoo her away. At the end of the song the half tabs open and* TINK *finally leaves.*)

WENDY   Where are the mermaids? I can't see any.

PETER   They must be further out. They only come ashore at high tide.

WENDY   I did so want to see a mermaid.

PETER   It's awfully difficult. They are such cruel creatures too — they will try to lure people into the water and drown them.

WENDY   How hateful!

PETER   This is a very hateful place — it's called Marooner's Bay. Sailors who commit crimes are tied up here while their ship sails away.

WENDY   How awful! You mean they are left high and dry?

PETER	Not for long! When the tide comes in, the beach is completely covered and that's the last of them.
WENDY	Ugh, I don't want to hear any more.
PETER	Wait! Listen!

(*Noises off, as of someone being dragged along.* PETER *and* WENDY *hide behind a rock set at the back of the stage.* SMEE, STARKEY *and the* SECOND TWIN *enter.*)

WENDY	Who's that with them?
PETER	It's Second Twin — they are going to maroon him.
SECOND TWIN	Oi! Stop shoving! There's no need to be so beastly.
SMEE	Sorry — we have to be rough, it's our raison d'etre. Anyway, the Captain insists on it. Are you ready for your swim — it will do you good to be clean for once.
SECOND TWIN	No! I haven't got my cossie. And I have been told to always keep my socks dry, that's why I never wash them.
SMEE	I'm sorry to hear that. Cleanliness is next to Godliness, you know.
STARKEY	Oh do shut it Smee. The sooner he drowns the sooner we get off duty.
WENDY	Poor boy!
STARKEY	What did you say?
SMEE	I didn't say a thing. I thought it was you, I told you those trousers were too tight for your own good.
STARKEY	You cheeky . . .

(*He takes a wild swipe at* SMEE, *who ducks.* SECOND TWIN *is not so lucky.*)

SECOND TWIN	Owwww! That hurt! Pick on someone your own size.
SMEE	Sorry. Nothing personal. That's us all over — violent but cheery. Well if it wasn't you Starkey, who was it?
PETER	(*imitating* HOOK'S *voice*) 'Twas me you fools!
STARKEY	'Tis the Cap'n!

SMEE	You're not wrong there — I mean aarrh, 'tis him.
STARKEY	We have the boy, Cap'n. He'll soon be no more.
PETER	Set him free!
SMEE	But Cap'n . . .
PETER	Do as I say, or 'twill be the worse for you both. Remember the hook!
SMEE	This is very odd. He never changes his mind. Inflexible is his middle name.
STARKEY	Really? I heard it was Cecil.
SMEE	Don't let him hear that, he hates it. We'd better follow orders.
STARKEY	You must be joking — we're supposed to do away with the boy.
SMEE	I've got a hunch.
STARKEY	You can get ointment for that.
SMEE	No, an idea! Let's ask the audience, they wouldn't lie to us. Should we let the boy go?
AUDIENCE	Yes!
STARKEY	Oh, no you shouldn't!
AUDIENCE SMEE SECOND TWIN }	Oh, yes we should!
SMEE	Seems clear cut to me. Off you go then.
	(He releases SECOND TWIN, *who runs off. The real* HOOK *is heard offstage.)*
HOOK	*(off)* Ahoy, lubbers! Where are ye? What's taking so long?
SMEE STARKEY }	*(looking at each other)* The Cap'n! But who . . .
	(HOOK *enters. He is not in a good mood.*)
AUDIENCE	Boo!

HOOK   Bah! Suffering seahorses!

STARKEY   What's up, Cap'n?

HOOK   Those boys have found a mother, someone to organise them. We are undone.

SMEE   Sorry, it's this bloomin' zip.

STARKEY   'Tis evil news.

SMEE   What's a mother?

WENDY   (*horrified*) He doesn't know what a mother is, poor lamb.

HOOK   What was that?

PETER   (*very unconvincingly*) Splash.

SMEE   Must be one of those mermaids.

HOOK   Smee! How many more times! 'Tis them mermaids!

STARKEY   Cap'n, could we not kidnap the boy's mother for ourselves?

HOOK   Blazing barnacles! Tis a princely idea. We will seize them boys, make them walk the plank and she will be our skivvy! The last outpost of true chauvinism!

WENDY   Never!

PETER   Splash.

            (*The* PIRATES *think for a moment, then shake their heads in unison.*)

HOOK   'Tis passing strange. I could swear I heard a voice. Never mind — what say you, my bully boys?

STARKEY   There's my hand on it.

SMEE   And mine too.

HOOK   And there is my hook. But I forgot. Where is the boy? Perished already?

SMEE   No, it's alright Cap'n, we let him go as you said.

HOOK	What's this? Let him go? By Long John Silver's parrot, what possessed you?
STARKEY	'Twas your own orders Cap'n.
SMEE	You called to us to let him go.
HOOK	Brimstone and gall! Lads, I gave no such order.
STARKEY	Then, 'tis passing queer — we heard your voice.
HOOK	Spirit that haunts this lagoon, dost hear me?
PETER	(*still imitating* HOOK) Odds, bobs, hammer and tongs. I hear you.
HOOK	Who are you, strange spirit?
PETER	I am Jas Hook. Captain of the Jolly Roger.
HOOK	You cannot be. I am that Captain, am I not boys?
SMEE STARKEY }	Indeed, you are that Cap'n.
HOOK	If you are Hook as you say, then pray, who am I?
PETER	A husk, an empty vessel, a Grecian urn.
HOOK	A Grecian urn? What's a Grecian urn?
ALL	About fifty quid a week!
HOOK	(*despairingly, to the audience*) And this passes for entertainment? What manner of thing are you?
PETER	Guess! Twenty questions!
HOOK	Vegetable?
PETER	No!
HOOK	Mineral?
PETER	No!
HOOK	Animal?
PETER	Aye! But what animal?

HOOK	Man! But something eludes me — I should know you.
PETER	Indeed you should — do you give up?
HOOK	Yes! Rot you!
PETER	Well then, I am your sworn enemy — Peter Pan!
HOOK	But of course! Take him dead or alive boys!

(PETER *leaps up, drawing his sword.* HOOK *motions* SMEE *and* STARKEY *to stay back.*)

| HOOK | Let me have him, I need no help to finish this upstart. |

(*They fight.*)

| HOOK | (*during a pause for breath*) Well fought, boy. But you will never best Jas Hook! |
| PETER | We shall see! |

(*They fight again.* PETER *whips* HOOK's *sword from his hand and forces* HOOK *to his knees.* HOOK *spreads his arms wide.*)

| HOOK | Come Pan, would you kill an unarmed man? Let us settle this like gentlemen in fair fight. |

(PETER *throws his sword aside and advances on* HOOK, *fists raised.*)

| PETER | I am surprised to hear you talk of fairness. |
| HOOK | And so you should be! Did you expect me to change my spots? |

(HOOK *stabs* PETER *with a knife concealed under his coat.* PETER *groans and collapses.*)

| WENDY | Peter! |
| HOOK | What a fool, falling for the oldest trick in the cheat's book! And as for you my pretty . . . |

(WENDY *snatches up the discarded sword and stands over* PETER.)

| WENDY | Leave me be! You will not find me easy prey! |
| HOOK | Foolish girl, thinking you can defy me. |

STARKEY   Leave her be Cap'n. The tide is coming in. It will save you the
                 trouble.

                 (HOOK *laughs in his most sinister way.*)

WENDY   I really don't see what you find so amusing.

HOOK   Starkey is right. It seems that I need not deal with you myself,
                 my dear. Stay with your fallen hero — within a few minutes
                 you will both be drowned. Come, my bully boys!

                 (HOOK *laughs, as the* PIRATES *leave.* WENDY *stands over* PETER
                 as the curtains close.)

                                    Scene Five

The half tabs are closed. We are in an unspecified part of Never Land. TINK
*sits sadly by herself. Song such as "When will I be loved", "In my life" or
"Sweet dreams". The song should reflect* TINK'S *feeling of being neglected in
favour of another.*

TINK   (*at end of song*) Oh, hello audience. I'm sorry you have found
                 me so depressed, but in my place I think you would feel the
                 same.

AUDIENCE   Aaaah . . .

TINK   You know my problem of course, it's that Wendy. Of all the
                 no good, sneaky man grabbers — she's the worst. Not that it's
                 her fault — in her place I would have been the same. It's just
                 that I'm Peter's fairy — always have been, always will be.
                 Mind you I've never had much success with men. I sent my
                 picture to a lonely hearts club, but they sent it back. They said
                 they weren't that lonely.

                 (*There are noises offstage.*)

TINK   What was that?

                 (HOOK *and the* PIRATES *enter.*)

AUDIENCE   Boo!

HOOK   Thank you fans. Grab her boys!

                 (*The* PIRATES *do so.*)

TINK   Let me go! Just you wait till Peter hears of this!

SMEE	Who is this?
HOOK	Don't you know her? Look at that face.
SMEE	Do I have to? I want danger money.
HOOK	It's Tinkerbell. Peter's fairy. So, Tink. Not feeling quite so brave now?
TINK	Me afraid? Rubbish! I don't care what you do to me — hot irons, thumbscrews, the rack. You won't make me talk.
HOOK	We are going to hurt you.
TINK	What do you want to know?
	(HOOK *thinks for a moment, then kicks her shin.*)
TINK	(*hopping wildly*) Owwww! No, no, really, I'll tell you anything. I was only joking.
	(HOOK *performs a side hair tweak on* TINK, *who falls to her knees.*)
TINK	Ahhhh!
HOOK	You don't understand. We don't really care what you tell us — we're going to hurt you anyway. Gratuitous violence is our trade mark.
SMEE	Oh come on. Cap'n. Give her a break. After all she's only a girl — and not too bad as they go. But then I'm not wearing my glasses.
HOOK	Smee. I really am rather disappointed in you.
	(*He advances on* SMEE, *hook raised.* SMEE *subsides, cowed.* TINK *throws herself in front of* HOOK.)
TINK	You really should listen to him, but I'll tell you anyway. Peter lives in a house deep in the forest, by the Evergreen Glade. He had it made for Wendy. It's the one that looks as if a bomb hit it.
HOOK	I hope you're taking notes, Smee.
TINK	You said you weren't interested in what I said!
HOOK	I lied, of course! Now hear this, Tinkerbell. Wendy and Peter are both dead — drowned in Marooner's Bay. And with your

information I can help their friends to join them. And you will be all alone! That's the price you pay for betraying your nearest and dearest. Goodbye! Hahahaha . . .

AUDIENCE   Boo!

HOOK   Leave her here to rot! We don't need her any more — come my bully boys!

(HOOK *and the* PIRATES *leave, singing a suitably piratey ditty, which fades away.*)

TINK   What a beast! What a bully! What choice did I have? I've been an ardent coward all my life. And anyway I don't believe Peter's dead — Hook would say that just to frighten me. I must find Peter and warn him that the search is on before it's too late. Wish me luck, audience!

(*The curtains close.*)

Scene Six

The shore of the Mermaid's Lagoon, once again. PETER *is lying where we left him.* WENDY *is cradling his head in her arms.*

PETER   Oooeaauaoo . . .

WENDY   Peter! You're alive!

(PETER *raises himself on one elbow and feels his chest.*)

PETER   I think I am. My chest hurts like the devil though. What happened?

WENDY   Hook stabbed you and left us on this beach to drown.

PETER   The tide must be coming in. How long have we got, do you think?

WENDY   Minutes, probably. We had better get out of here if we can. Shall we swim or fly?

PETER   I don't mind what you do, Wendy.

WENDY   What do you mean, "you"?

PETER   I don't think I can even stand. It is the stab wound — I think I must be dying.

WENDY   The water will probably get us first.

PETER   Well that's a relief! At least I won't die of anything serious.

                (PETER *realises that* WENDY *has not moved*.)

PETER   Wendy! You must be going!

WENDY   I'm staying with you.

PETER   What? You must go! If you leave now, you will just escape the
                tide.

WENDY   I probably wouldn't.

PETER   But you might!

WENDY   I don't care! I'm not leaving you.

PETER   Is this how mothers behave?

WENDY   Oh, Peter!

PETER   I'm sorry. What did I say? Listen, I can hear something.

                (*There is the clumping sound of approaching feet.*)

WENDY   Who can it be?

PETER   It's Tink! I would recognise those feet anywhere.

WENDY   Oh no! But I suppose she might be of some use.

                (TINK *enters in her usual subtle manner*.)

TINK   What are you two doing here? Hook told me you were dead,
                Peter. I've been going frantic with worry. And I find you here
                having a sneaky kip! I've been wearing myself out searching
                high and low — I don't know why I bother, really I don't!

PETER   I'm sorry Tink, but the last thing I need now is a lecture. You
                could at least be a little sympathetic.

TINK   Why, what's wrong with you?

WENDY   He's been stabbed. He fought Hook to save me, but Hook
                cheated as usual and now Peter's dying . . . (*She starts to cry.*)

TINK   Is that all! Do stop that noise, I can't hear myself think.

WENDY   If it was as silent as a monastery, you still couldn't hear yourself think! Didn't you hear? I said he's dying.

TINK   Yes, I did hear the first time. But there's no need to panic. I can cure him — all we need is some of my magic.

PETER   I don't like the sound of that. The cure is likely to be worse than the wound.

WENDY   I've seen your magic at work — you'll only make it worse.

TINK   Oh, no I won't! You just watch this, oh ye of little faith!

Abracadabra, alikazam,
Chocolate drops and strawberry jam,
Now in place of scenes of strife
What we need is signs of life.

(TINK *sprinkles some of her fairy dust, in an expansive gesture. Nothing happens except everyone chokes. Silence.*)

WENDY   What did I tell you!

TINK   That was just a rehearsal! I'll do it this time.

(TINK *repeats the verse and sprinkles more dust. A large multicoloured plant grows from behind the rock and all the stage lights go green.*)

WENDY   Well, that's real progress, I must say!

TINK   Oh, you're such a know-all. This time all or nothing!

(*Repeat verse and dust. This time there is a flash and a triumphant chord. The plant disappears and all the lights come up.*)

PETER   (*slowly sitting up*) By George, she's done it. I think she's done it! It doesn't hurt any more.

TINK   See, told you so!

(*She bows to the audience and encourages clapping, cutting this off and re-starting with suitable gestures.*)

WENDY   Well done Tink. I take it all back, you can do magic. But why were you looking for us — what's happened?

TINK   Weeell — it's like this. I was surprised by Hook and the pirates. They tortured me, because they wanted to know where

the boys are. They used all sorts of terrible methods and it
went on for hours. But being the dependable fairy I am, I
gritted my teeth and held out against the worst they could do.
Then they told me you were dead. I didn't believe it and I still
didn't tell.

PETER   What nothing?

TINK   Well hardly anything, although they were awfully rough.

PETER   I have to say it — you don't look that distressed. More like a
           fashion victim than a torture victim. What did you really tell
           them?

TINK   Only a few little snippets, just to keep them happy. Just where
           the house was, and how many boys there are, and the best
           method to achieve a surprise, and when they are most likely to
           be off their guard — just a few things.

PETER   Oh, Tink! How could you?

TINK   Don't blame me, I couldn't help it. I'm tough — but I'm
           cowardly tough, if you know what I mean.

WENDY   What shall we do, Peter? They will all be captured and
           slaughtered.

PETER   We must get to them before Hook does. Now, before it's too
           late. We can still just beat the tide if we go now.

           (*There is the sound of the* PIRATES *in the distance, singing
           their piratey song.*)

PETER   Not a moment to lose. They are coming this way! Follow me!

WENDY }
TINK   }   We're coming — wait for us!

           (*All exit as the curtain falls.*)

ACT TWO

Scene One

In front of half tabs. HOOK *and the* PIRATES *enter and sing a song of suspect morality. This is an opportunity for some suitable choreography. Possibly "Never Get Caught", from Treasure Island by Hal Shaper and Cyril Ornandel.*

HOOK   (*as the song ends*) Yes, that's the spirit lads, that's what I like to hear! Now for this lot. Hello audience! Did you enjoy your little drinkies in the interval? I hope so, because it's probably the last thing you will enjoy! I suppose you think that Peter's won? Yes? He may be still alive, but I'm not finished yet — I know where he lives now! And if he isn't ready when I come knocking, that's his own look out! My merry lads and I are off to deal with Peter and his cronies once and for all — and when we've finished with them, we'll be back for you lot! So — you had better beware. Goodbye — for now!

      (HOOK *and the* PIRATES *march off, to the refrain of "Never Get Caught".*)

Scene Two

The half tabs open to reveal the interior of the Tree House — again, this is an opportunity for inventiveness in creating an apparently underground room. If this creates difficulties, the same setting as used in Act One, Scene Three will suffice. WENDY, JOHN, MICHAEL *and all the* LOST BOYS *are creating domestic bliss.*

MICHAEL   Tell uth the storwy you promithed.

WENDY   Once you have done your lessons. Come along, settle down.

      (*They sit cross legged, in a semi-circle around* WENDY.)

WENDY   First question. History. Name two British queens named Elizabeth.

SECOND TWIN   Elizabeth first and eleventh.

WENDY   Second! Maths. If you had seven pounds in one pocket and seven pounds in the other pocket, what would you have?

MICHAEL   Thomeone elthe's twowtherth on.

WENDY	No. Try again. If you had five bars of chocolate and Captain Hook asked you for one, how many would you have left?
CURLY	Five!
WENDY	Terrible, terrible . . . how many boys are there?
SLIGHTLY	Seven.
WENDY	Seven? Don't you mean eight?
JOHN	No, Michael doesn't count.
MICHAEL	I don't wead or wite either.
WENDY	I don't believe this. How did you all get so stupid?
FIRST TWIN	Practice.
WENDY	Did any of you Lost Boys go to school?
TOOTLES	I went to medical school.
WENDY	You? What did you study?
NIBS	Nothing, they studied him!
WENDY	Good grief. Didn't anyone else go to school?
SLIGHTLY	I did. I was very advanced. I was thirteen but the other children were only six!
WENDY	Oh, I give up. Story time.
ALL	Hooray! We win again!
WENDY	Well, there was once a gentleman . . .
FIRST TWIN	No one we know then.
WENDY	Be quiet! There was also a lady. They were called Mr and Mrs Darling.
JOHN	I remember them.
MICHAEL	I think I wemember them.
TOOTLES	What were they like?

WENDY	Oh, just an ordinary couple you know. But they were very special to their children.
SLIGHTLY	What did Mr Darling do?
WENDY	He was a soldier. He fought with Gordon at Khartoum, with Baden Powell and Redvers Buller in South Africa. He fought with Kitchener and Haig — he didn't get on with anyone really.
CURLY	How long was he a soldier?
WENDY	He wore Her Majesty's uniform for thirty five years.
SECOND TWIN	Of course, it fitted her better.
NIBS	Is this going to be a horrible story?
WENDY	Certainly not!
JOHN	Shame!
CURLY	I know an unsuitable story! There was an Englishman, an Irishman and a Scotsman . . .
WENDY	No! We are not going to hear that story! Anyway, Mr and Mrs Darling had three children, but one day Peter Pan came and the children flew away to the Never Land where the Lost Boys are.
TOOTLES	Was one of the boys called Tootles?
WENDY	Yes he was.
TOOTLES	I'm in a story, I'm in a story!
WENDY	However, consider the feelings of the unhappy parents with their children flown away. Think of the empty beds.
FIRST TWIN	They should fill them with flowers and make flower beds.
SECOND TWIN	This story is awfully sad. Ha ha ha.
	(PETER *enters quietly and stands to one side listening.*)
WENDY	Years roll by, but who is this elegant lady of an uncertain age alighting at Paddington Station? Can it be . . . yes . . . no . . . yes, it is the fair Wendy!
TOOTLES	Hooray!

WENDY	And who are these handsome, distinguished men with her? Can it be John and Michael?
CURLY	Not likely!
WENDY	Yes, they are. "See dear brothers" says Wendy, pointing upward. "There is the window standing open". So up they fly to the relieved and welcoming arms of their parents, and everyone lives happily ever after.
PETER	Hmmmph!
WENDY	Peter? Is something wrong?
PETER	Wendy, you are wrong about mothers. I thought like you about the window so I stayed away for moons and moons, but when I flew back the window was barred. My mother had forgotten about me and another little boy was sleeping in my bed.

(Everyone becomes most alarmed.)

JOHN	Wendy, we must go home!
WENDY	Are you sure mothers are like that?
PETER	Absolutely.
FIRST TWIN	You're not leaving, Wendy?
WENDY	I fear I must.
TOOTLES	We won't let you go!
WENDY	Then come with me! I'm sure I could get mother and father to adopt you. Come on, get ready!

(Everybody scurries about, collecting their few belongings. PETER *folds his arms and turns his back.)*

WENDY	Peter, get your clothes.
PETER	I'm not going with you, Wendy.
WENDY	What? Think of the dangers — you can't stay here alone!
PETER	Yes I can.
WENDY	No you can't!

PETER   Yes I can! Don't care anyway.

WENDY   Boys, Peter isn't coming!

JOHN   Not coming?

CURLY   Why not?

PETER   I just want to be a boy and have fun.

WENDY   You won't come even for me?

PETER   No, not even for you. I don't care about anyone except me.

WENDY   (*with sudden hostility*) No you don't, do you?

PETER   Pardon?

WENDY   You really don't care, you haven't got any finer feelings. All
            you can think of is having fun. You're not going to grow up —
            I can see you being a selfish little brat when you are eighty
            years old!

PETER   Right — that's it!

            (*He starts to go.* WENDY *instantly relents.*)

WENDY   Peter, don't go! Look, I'm sorry. I didn't mean it.

PETER   Goodbye, I hope you all enjoy your mothers.

            (*He exits in a huff.*)

WENDY   Peter, you've forgotten your medicine.

            (*She waves a small flask forlornly, then drops it in a
            prominent place. The lights go down leaving* WENDY *picked
            out in a spotlight. Song, such as "Something" by the Beatles,
            "These Foolish Things", "Sweet Dreams" etc. The boys join
            in as appropriate. At the end of the song* FIRST TWIN *sees
            something offstage.*)

FIRST TWIN I think Peter's coming back.

            (*Everyone scrambles to see.*)

SECOND TWIN No, I don't think it's Peter. He doesn't have a hook!

NIBS   Whoops, we'd better move fast.

CURLY   I agree, but where to?

NIBS   South America!

                (HOOK *and the* PIRATES *enter from all sides.*)

HOOK   Too late! I have you now!

AUDIENCE   Boo!

HOOK   Thank you!

WENDY   Leave the talking to me. Just try to look intelligent.

SLIGHTLY   Oh, dear.

WENDY   Leave us alone Hook. You are standing on our domain.

HOOK   How very painful for you!

JOHN   Do not jest. We know people willing to drive you out of the
                country at any price.

HOOK   Oh, yes? And who might that be?

MICHAEL   Taxthe dwivers!

HOOK   Silence!

SMEE   Yes, we were hoping for a laugh there.

HOOK   Where is Peter Pan?

CURLY   He went away because Wendy called him a selfish little brat.

HOOK   How right you are, my dear. But he'll be back I wager. (*He
                notices the flask.*) What is that, my dear?

WENDY   (*snatching it up*) Er, um . . . it's . . .

HOOK   It's Peter's, isn't it? It's his medicine isn't it? Grab it, lads!

                (SMEE *grabs* WENDY's *hand and removes the flask gently. He
                gives it to* HOOK.)

HOOK   He'll be back and he'll drink it — because he's a good little
                boy! And when he does he'll be poisoned to death!

                (HOOK *drops tablets into the flask, and puts it in plain view.*)

WENDY	You fiend! Why do you want to kill Peter?
HOOK	Because he's a vicious little monster and a pain in the . . .
WENDY	Nonsense, he's just highly strung.
HOOK	You couldn't string him high enough for me. Right, my jolly dogs, to the ship. We mustn't keep johnny plank waiting. Ha ha ha ha . . .

(The PIRATES *march* WENDY *and the boys offstage, perhaps singing a chorus or two of "Never get caught".* TINK, *who has been surreptitiously watching from the other side, enters.)*

TINK	Gordon Bennett! They're in trouble and no mistake. If only I could have got here sooner, I could have foiled those pirates single handed — I'm the toughest fairy that ever lived. Why I dealt with the hippy cannibal, who ate three squares a day. Hook's a good deal worse though, what with kidnapping, torture and murder. There ought to be a law against people like him. Why, if my old mother could see me now, associating with people like him, she'd be so ashamed. She thinks I'm in prison.

*(*PETER *returns, looking somewhat sheepish.)*

PETER	Wendy? Wendy, I'm sorry I went off like that. Oh, it's you — I thought you were Wendy. I must get my eyes tested.
TINK	Peter, I've got some bad news.
PETER	I can take it.
TINK	I've got a lot of bad news.
PETER	Have you got a list?
TINK	No, I always stand like this. Oh, I see. Peter, the pirates have captured Wendy and all the boys.
PETER	No! We must rescue her.
TINK	Her?
PETER	And the boys too, of course.
TINK	You pay far too much attention to that Wendy.
PETER	She's a very nice girl, for a girl.

TINK	Nice? She blunts one's conception of man as natures' final word.
PETER	I wish you and Wendy would get on.
TINK	Oh, we will given time. I've bought her a present.
PETER	That's splendid. What is it?
TINK	It's a beautiful chair. All I need now is somewhere to plug it in. Be careful of her, Peter. She's dangerous.
PETER	Dangerous?
TINK	She wants to make a man of you. She wants to get her hooks into you, just as much as the Captain does.

(Cue for a song, such as "Don't Go Breaking My Heart", sung as a duet.)

PETER	Now that's settled, we'd better try to rescue them.
TINK	Don't worry, I'll stand by you.
PETER	I'm very touched.
TINK	Don't be. You just make me look tall!
PETER	Before we go is there anything we need? Of course! My medicine! Just the thing to give me strength — I shall need all I can get.

(PETER *picks up the flask.*)

TINK	Stop it! What are you doing?
PETER	I'm going to take my medicine.
TINK	But you mustn't! Hook has poisoned it!
PETER	Poisoned? Ridiculous. Of course it isn't.
TINK	Oh, yes it is!
PETER	Oh, no it isn't!
TINK AUDIENCE }	Oh, yes it is!

(*All this time* TINK *is vainly trying to wrest the flask from* PETER.)

PETER   This is nonsense. I promised Wendy that I would take it, and I will.

TINK   Right. Look out! Hook's behind you!

PETER   I don't believe that either.

TINK   But he is, I tell you. Isn't he audience?

(*She encourages the audience, nodding madly.*)

AUDIENCE   Yes!

PETER   What? Help!

(*He looks away.* TINK *grabs the flask from him, drinks the entire contents, then throws the flask offstage.*)

PETER   Oi! You've drunk all my medicine.

TINK   Bright lad.

(TINK *begins to sway and goes into a prolonged and melodramatic stage "death".* PETER *watches helplessly and kneels by her side as she finally falls in a heap. He takes her hand.*)

PETER   It was poisoned — and yet you drank it to save me! Tink, dear Tink, are you dying?

TINK   (*weakly*) Yes.

PETER   I feel so helpless. Is there nothing I can do?

TINK   (*even more weakly*) I can only get well again if people believe in fairies.

PETER   Did you hear that audience?

AUDIENCE   Yes.

PETER   Tink will only get well if you lot believe in fairies. Well, go on! Say, "We believe in fairies". Now!

AUDIENCE   (*almost certainly mumbling*) We believe in fairies.

PETER   Oh, good grief! That's pathetic. Once again — "We believe in
             fairies".

AUDIENCE   We believe in fairies.

PETER   Louder! I know you're out there, I heard you snoring. Again.
             One, two, three.

AUDIENCE   We believe in fairies!

PETER   She's slightly better, but you're still not loud enough. One last
             time. One, two, three.

AUDIENCE   We believe in fairies!!

             (TINK *stretches, opens her eyes and slowly stands up.* PETER
             helps her up and dusts her down.)

TINK   That was horrible, but I'm all right now thanks to them.

PETER   It worked! It really worked. Thank you, thank you! Amazing
             how silly adults can be. Now off to rescue Wendy and the
             boys! Wish us luck!

             (PETER *and* TINK *exit at high speed, waving.*)

                             Scene Three

In front of half tabs. SMEE *enters with a musket on his shoulder.*

SMEE   Hello, audience. Nice to see you. Are you all enjoying
             yourselves?

AUDIENCE   Yes!

SMEE   Why? What are you doing? Seriously though audience, I'm in
             a bit of bother. Will you give me a hand?

AUDIENCE   Yes.

SMEE   That's very good of you. You see, Captain Hook has told me to
             guard the ship, but it's very big and I can't watch it all by
             myself. So, if I'm not here and you see the crocodile, shout
             "There's a crocodile, Mr Smee!". Got that?

AUDIENCE   Yes.

SMEE   Good. Let's have a practice. One, two, three . . .

AUDIENCE There's a crocodile, Mr Smee!

SMEE Brilliant! I'm just going to check round the back now, so you keep watch.

(SMEE exits. There is a silence, then a faint sound of ticking, which gets louder. The CROCODILE enters.)

AUDIENCE There's a crocodile, Mr. Smee!

(The CROCODILE hides, the ticking fades and SMEE runs on, out of breath.)

SMEE Where is it? Where is it? There's nothing here. You've tricked me, haven't you?

AUDIENCE No.

SMEE Hmmmph! You'd better not. Well, I'm off round the back again. Keep a good look out.

(SMEE exits, and the CROCODILE duly returns, still ticking.)

AUDIENCE There's a crocodile, Mr Smee!

(The CROCODILE hides, the ticking fades and SMEE runs on, even more out of breath. He looks everywhere, but of course sees nothing.)

SMEE Alright, I get it! You are having me on again. It's be nasty to Smee day, is it? It's not nice to tease a poor innocent pirate, you know.

(He exits and the CROCODILE returns. The ticking continues from now until TINK puts her head in its mouth.)

AUDIENCE There's a crocodile, Mr Smee!

(SMEE re-enters and the CROCODILE hides behind him.)

SMEE You'd better be right this time! Well, where is it?

AUDIENCE He's behind you!

SMEE Behind me? Never. I'll prove it.

(SMEE stalks round the stage in a big circle. The CROCODILE follows him closely, matching stride for stride.)

SMEE *(stopping at the front of the stage)* See. No crocodiles.

(*The* CROCODILE *puts a napkin around his neck, pulls out a knife and fork, and prepares to eat* SMEE.)

AUDIENCE   He's behind you!

SMEE   Oh, no he isn't!

AUDIENCE   Oh, yes he is!

SMEE   Oh, no he isn't! I'll prove it.

(*The* CROCODILE *ducks as* SMEE *turns round slowly.*)

SMEE   There I told you. No crocodile.

(*The* CROCODILE *stands up.*)

AUDIENCE   He's behind you!

(SMEE *turns round and sees the* CROCODILE.)

SMEE   Aaaah! Nice crocodile! Stay calm, Smee!

(*The* CROCODILE *gently removes the musket from* SMEE'S *grasp and pushes him to his knees.*)

SMEE   Heeellllp!

(PETER *and* TINK *enter. The* CROCODILE *turns to face them.*)

SMEE   Thank goodness you've come! Oh, dear — Peter Pan.

PETER   Why, it's a pirate! Good work crocodile. Carry on, don't mind us.

(*The* CROCODILE *goes back to* SMEE *and stands over him, guarding his dinner.*)

TINK   What are you doing? Save him, Peter!

PETER   Why?

TINK   Um. Because . . . because . . . it's not nice to kill anyone.

PETER   But he's a pirate.

TINK   He's a nice pirate. It's Smee — he tried to help me.

PETER   Oh, alright. Crocodile, come here!

(*The* Crocodile *leaves* Smee *and goes to* Peter.)

PETER   If you don't eat Smee, then I will do something for you.

TINK   What?

PETER   I'll stop his clock from ticking.

(*The* Crocodile *becomes greatly excited.*)

TINK   How can you do that?

PETER   Well, for a start, I'll need your help.

TINK   Mine?

PETER   Yes. Now you know you are ugly . . .

TINK   Me? Ugly? How dare you!

PETER   Come on, you know you are. When you walk into a room the mice jump on chairs. Your face could stop a clock — his clock.

(TINK *is speechless for some time, her mouth opening and shutting.*)

TINK   How . . . how?

PETER   Easy. You just put your head in the crocodile's mouth.

TINK   You have to be joking! ·

PETER   Fine. Crocodile — Tink says no. Carry on and eat Smee.

TINK   But . . . but . . . it won't work!

PETER   Of course it will. Audience, do you think Tink should give it a try?

AUDIENCE   Yes!

TINK   Well, alright . . .

(TINK *gingerly puts her head in the* Crocodile's *mouth. The ever present ticking falters, stops. There is a final* "*sproyoyong*". *Silence.*)

PETER   It worked! I told you so! Off you go, crocodile. You are free to pursue Hook, unheard and unlooked for. Back to the good times!

                        (*There is an opportunity here to introduce another song, "Crocodile Rock", if desired. The* CROCODILE *skips round the stage happily and exits to the music.*)

PETER   Happy, Tink? Now for Hook!

TINK   You go ahead. I'll catch you up.

PETER   Righto. Don't be long.

                        (PETER *exits and* TINK *sidles up to* SMEE.)

TINK   Hello sailor. My name is Tinkerbell.

SMEE   That's not my fault.

TINK   What's it like being a pirate?

SMEE   It's a living.

TINK   Why did you become a pirate, anyway?

SMEE   They sent me on the pirate's youth training scheme.

TINK   There's no future in it you know. I can't remember any pirates who lived to enjoy their ill-gotten gains. Blackbeard was hung from the yard arm, Hawkins was eaten by cannibals, Long John was marooned . . .

SMEE   Don't rub it in! It wasn't my first choice you know. I used to be an organist, but someone stole my monkey.

TINK   So you quit?

SMEE   I left after something my boss said.

TINK   Why, what did he say?

SMEE   "You're fired".

TINK   What a silly man. I think you are lovely.

SMEE   Really? I think you are lovely, too.

TINK   Stout fellow.

SMEE	You're a stout fellow, too. You could make two of me.
TINK	I'll make two of you! Where's an axe?
SMEE	No, only joking. I think I love you, Tinkerbell.
TINK	Oh, Smee . . . will you love me when I am old and ugly?
SMEE	Of course I do! Marry me!
TINK	Yes! Yes! Yes! I feel more attractive already. Do you think I'll lose my looks with age?
SMEE	If you are lucky.
TINK	And they say romance is dead!
SMEE	I don't care what you look like. Beauty is in the eye of the beholder and you look good to me!

(Cue for a duet, such as "You're The One That I Want". TINK and SMEE embrace as the curtains close.)

Scene Four

During the last scene, the setting has been changed to the deck of the Pirate Ship, complete with rails and an entrance to the cabin. As the half tabs and curtains open, HOOK and the PIRATES appear on stage, all except SMEE.

HOOK	Victory! Victory is mine at last! Where are the boys?
JUKES	We have them here, Captain.
HOOK	Hoist them up.
STARKEY	Tumble up, you ungentlemanly lubbers!

(The boys are pushed onstage from the cabin.)

NIBS	Promise you won't hurt us! Promise!
HOOK	Very well. You won't feel a thing.
NIBS	I wish I was dead.
HOOK	It's your lucky day, your wish is about to come true.
SLIGHTLY	You can't do this to us, we have rights!

HOOK	Like?
SLIGHTLY	We have the right to remain silent!
HOOK	Yes. As long as you can stand the pain.
SECOND TWIN	Let us go. I warn you, we are desperate men.
HOOK	You should have gone before you came out. Now, keep quiet before I blow your brains out.
JOHN	That shouldn't take long.
HOOK	Silence! Seven of you must walk the plank tonight, but I have room for a cabin boy. Which of you is it to be?
TOOTLES	I don't think my mother would like me to be a pirate, sir. Would your mother like you to be a pirate, Slightly?
SLIGHTLY	I don't think so. Would your mother like you to be a pirate, Curly?
CURLY	I don't think so. Would your mother . . .
HOOK	Stow this gab, you mother's boys. (*To* JOHN.) You, boy — you look as if you had a little pluck in you. Did you never want to be a pirate?
JOHN	What would you call me if I joined?
HOOK	Boy!
JOHN	What do you think, Michael?
MICHAEL	Would he sthill be a wespecthful thubjecth of the Queen?
HOOK	He would have to swear, "down with the Queen".
MICHAEL	Then he wefuthes.
JOHN	Then I refuth — I mean refuse!
HOOK	That seals your fate. Bring up their mother!
	(WENDY *is dragged onstage from the cabin.*)
HOOK	Just in time my dear, to see these boys walk the plank.
WENDY	Then they will die like true British gentlemen. But you will kill them for nothing!

HOOK	It's most generous. We normally make a charge.
WENDY	Is there nothing I can do to save them? I'd do anything.
HOOK	Nothing! Oh, I don't know though.
SECOND TWIN	Captain, may we have one last request? You can't deny us that.
HOOK	True, 'tis the unwritten law.
NIBS	We want Wendy to sing us a song to cheer us up.
BOYS	Yes!
HOOK	Very well. Get on with it, girl!

(WENDY *proceeds to sing "There's No Place Like Home", with the boys humming along and introducing appropriate gestures. The* PIRATES *are collectively overcome and burst into tears, blowing noses, etc, as the song ends.*)

HOOK	That's quite enough of that! Now try shouting "help".

(*A loud ticking comes from offstage.*)

STARKEY	It's him! It's the crocodile!

(*The* PIRATES *scatter offstage.* PETER *and* SMEE *enter, unseen by the* PIRATES. PETER *is making the ticking noise — he puts his finger to his lips for the benefit of the boys.*)

PETER	Shhh! Thanks, Smee.
SMEE	You are still not out of the woods — remember, if there is anything more I can do?
PETER	You have done enough. Look out! They are coming back.
SMEE	It is gone, Captain! There is not a sound.

(PETER *goes into the cabin. The* PIRATES *return and* WENDY *is taken to the back of the stage under guard.*)

HOOK	Gone! Saved by Davy Jones! Ah, Smee, back at last are we? Just in time — get the plank. No — wait! I think these boys need a taste of the lash first.
SECOND TWIN	No thanks, mum said we mustn't eat between meals.

HOOK   Fetch the cat, Jukes. It is in the cabin.

JUKES   Aye, aye, Cap'n.

                (JUKES *goes into the cabin. After a few seconds there is a
                strangled cry, followed by a triumphant crowing noise from*
                PETER.)

HOOK   What was that, by thunder?

SLIGHTLY   One down, six to go.

                (CECCO *looks into the cabin and backs out speedily.*)

HOOK   What's the matter with Bill Jukes, you dog?

CECCO   He's dead! Stabbed to the heart!

HOOK   Dead?

CECCO   The cabin's as black as the pit, but something terrible lurks in
                there. You heard it crowing!

HOOK   Cecco, go back then and fetch me that doodle-doo.

CECCO   Me, Cap'n? I think not.

HOOK   (*silkily*) Did you say you would go, Cecco?

                (CECCO *edges slowly into the cabin. All listen. One more
                strangled cry, one more crow.*)

TOOTLES   Two down, five to go.

HOOK   S'death and oddsfish! Who will bring me that doodle-doo?

STARKEY   We'll wait till Cecco comes out.

HOOK   I think I heard you volunteer, Starkey?

STARKEY   Not me, by thunder!

HOOK   My hook thinks you did. I wonder if it would not be advisable,
                to humour the hook?

STARKEY   I'll swing before I set foot in that cabin!

HOOK   So, is it mutiny? And Starkey is the ringleader! Shake hands,
                Starkey!

(STARKEY *recoils from the hook.* HOOK *stalks after him. They reach the rails and* HOOK *lunges.* STARKEY *falls over the rail. There is a short silence followed by a splash.*)

CURLY	Three down, four to go.
HOOK	Did any other gentleman think of mutiny?

(*The remaining* PIRATES *indicate that they did not even know the late* STARKEY.)

HOOK	As usual, if you want something done properly . . . I will bring out the doodle-doo!

(HOOK *enters the cabin, hook and knife at the ready. The door closes. It opens again almost at once and* HOOK *backs out, no longer holding his knife.*)

HOOK	Something struck the knife from my hand!
COOKSON	What of Cecco?
HOOK	As dead as Jukes.
COOKSON	They say the devil always boards a pirate ship at the last.
MULLINS	They say he comes in the likeness of the wickedest man on board.
COOKSON	Has he a hook, Cap'n?

(*The* PIRATES *are thoroughly frightened, the boys are enjoying themselves hugely.* HOOK *rounds on them.*)

HOOK	Do you like this, my bullies? I believe you do! Here is a pretty notion — we shall open the cabin door and drive you in. You can fight the doodle-doo for your lives. If you kill it we are so much the better. If he kills you, we are none the worse.
BOYS	Help! Mercy!

(*The boys are driven into the cabin. There is a long silence then more crowing.*)

MULLINS	The doodle-doo has killed them all!
COOKSON	The ship is bewitched!

HOOK	I have it lads, there is a Jonah aboard.
MULLINS	Aye, a man with a hook!
HOOK	No, not me lads. 'Tis the girl. There has never been good luck on a ship with a woman aboard.
SMEE	I don't believe it! She can do no harm.
COOKSON	It's worth a try. We have nothing to lose.
HOOK	Then throw the girl overboard.
MULLINS	There is none can save you now, missy!
PETER	(*from the cabin*) Wrong! Help is at hand.
HOOK	Who comes here?

(PETER *enters, sword drawn.*)

PETER	It is I, Peter Pan. Prepare to meet your doom!
HOOK	Hellfire and brimstone!
PETER	How dare you swear in front of Wendy!
HOOK	I'm sorry, I didn't know it was her turn. How did you get here?
PETER	By use of a very cunning plan.
HOOK	Stow it! Come my hearties, cleave him to the brisket!
PETER	Up boys, and at 'em!

(SMEE *surrenders immediately.* HOOK, MULLINS *and* COOKSON *make a fight of it, which rages all around the auditorium.* MULLINS *and* COOKSON *are overwhelmed and* HOOK *is cornered on the stage. The boys surround* HOOK, *who sweeps his hook in circles, keeping them back.*)

HOOK	Back, you scum!
PETER	Hold up, boys. This man is mine.
HOOK	So, Pan, this is all your doing?
PETER	Aye, Hook, 'tis all my doing.

HOOK	Proud and insolent youth, prepare to die!
PETER	Dark and sinister man, have at thee!
	(*They fight.*)
	You cannot win, Hook.
HOOK	Watch me!
PETER	But the villain cannot win.
HOOK	I shall rewrite the script.
PETER	Never! We shall have our happy ending!
HOOK	Yes — my happy ending! The villain gets the girl.
	(HOOK *abandons the fight and grabs* WENDY.)
HOOK	I believe the balance has shifted. Drop your sword!
	(PETER *obeys.*)
PETER	You cannot get away with this. Surrender, while you have time.
HOOK	Are you not supposed to say, "and let the girl go"?
PETER	Oh, yes, that too. I say again — surrender!
HOOK	Never! I shall escape to fight another day, you will never be free of fear of me!
PETER	I shall take the risk. Now free Wendy!
HOOK	Never!
	(*Unseen by* HOOK, *the now silent* CROCODILE *has appeared behind him.*)
PETER	Look behind you! The crocodile!
HOOK	You don't think that I would fall for that old trick do you? You are a bigger fool than I thought.
PETER	It is true, he is behind you. Is he not, audience?
AUDIENCE	Yes!

HOOK   I don't believe them any more than you. They are softies, and
                therefore on your side.

                (*The* Crocodile *taps him gently on the shoulder.* Hook *lets*
                Wendy *fall to the floor and turns slowly round.*)

HOOK   Aaarrgghh!

                (Hook *runs around the stage, closely pursued by the*
                Crocodile. *He is almost caught but finally escapes to the*
                wings. The Crocodile *rubs his hands, gives a skip, and*
                follows Hook *off. There is a respectful silence.*)

SMEE   He wasn't such a bad sort you know. I'd say he was one of the
                finest dead men ever to walk the earth.

MICHAEL   Ith Hook gone?

CURLY   He's gone.

SECOND TWIN   Where?

JOHN   We can't be completely sure, but he has a choice of two
                places.

WENDY   Are we safe now?

PETER   Yes, it is all over.

ALL   Hurrah!

                (*The curtains close.*)

                              Scene Five

The curtains open to half tabs. Enter Tink *and* Smee.

TINK   Hello, audience! Are you in a good mood?

AUDIENCE   Yes!

TINK   Lovely, now lend me a fiver.

SMEE   Er, you may be wondering what we are doing here?

TINK   I've certainly been wondering what we are doing here. Could
                it be that we are about to continue with an age old tradition?
                You know what has to happen now?

SMEE	Thank you, Tinkerbell. We are here to cheer you up, whether you like it or not.
TINK	Could be tricky, I saw you lot walking in! Anyhow, remember the last panto and all the ones before that? We had a jolly singalong, didn't we? So — it's your turn for some work. On behalf of the dramatic society . . .
SMEE	Because we are not taking the blame.
TINK	We are proud to present the audience participation song. Bring on the words, boys.

(The boys enter with the words of the chosen song.)

TINK	Wonderful. Now remember you are here to enjoy yourselves, so don't get crotchety.
SMEE	That was a joke, in case you hadn't noticed.
TINK	Wait a minute! They've given us the wrong song.
SMEE	No, it's just that the other one has been banned.
TINK	Shame! Anyway audience, remember to sing up.
SMEE	Yes, nice and loud, or we'll summon Hook back from the dead to give you a bit of an incentive.
TINK	Also, we will have a competition to see who can sing the loudest. The first prize is a week's holiday with me.
SMEE	*(aside)* The second prize is two week's holiday with her. *(To audience.)* Anyhow, let's go maestro. After three. Three.
TINK	Too slow, too slow!
SMEE	We'll try again. One, two, three . . .

(Song. Perhaps "Never Smile at A Crocodile". As usual, the audience will be cajoled into singing. As the song ends the boys exit, leaving TINK and SMEE on stage.)

SMEE	Well done, all of you. Now we shall leave you to find out what happens next, while we get to know each other better.
TINK	Smee, I am proud of you. You are a reformed pirate.

SMEE   I know, I went to reform school. Now, my fine fairy, put me
                under your spell. (*They embrace.*) Oi! Close the curtains, this
                is private!

                (*The curtains close.*)

                              Scene Six

The Nursery as in Act One, Scene One. MR *and* MRS DARLING *are sitting on
chairs, in semi darkness.*

MR DARLING   It's very quiet, Mary.

MRS DARLING   Oh, George!

MR DARLING   But then it's quiet every night. I thought I could get used to it
                — that I would enjoy it. But I can't and I don't!

MRS DARLING   I know, dear. I still can't believe that they are gone. Oh, what
                are we to do?

                (*She buries her head in a hanky. There is a small scratching
                noise and* NANA *barks offstage.*)

MRS DARLING   I wonder what has disturbed Nana?

MR DARLING   I don't hear anything.

MRS DARLING   You are right, of course. There can't be anyone outside.

MR DARLING   It's getting cold Mary, shut the window would you?

MRS DARLING   Oh, no George, don't ask me to do that. The window must
                always be left open for our children. Always.

MR DARLING   Very well, dear. But I am afraid I don't hold out much hope
                after all this time.

MRS DARLING   What was that, George?

MR DARLING   Nothing, dear. Go to sleep. Goodnight.

MRS DARLING   Goodnight.

                (*There is silence while they doze off. After a while* PETER *and*
                TINK *appear at the window.*)

PETER   They are asleep. Close the window, Tink. When Wendy comes
                back she will think her mother has locked her out, and then

she will come back with me. (*Pause.*) I thought I told you to close the window?

TINK   Yes. Yes, you did.

(PETER *studies* MRS DARLING, *forgetting about the window.* TINK *does nothing.*)

PETER   Poor Wendy's mother. You will never see Wendy again, lady, for the window will be barred!

TINK   She's been crying, Peter.

PETER   She must be very fond of Wendy. Well, I'm fond of her too and we can't both have her.

TINK   Peter, we must leave the window open. You know we must!

PETER   But, I don't want Wendy to . . . I mean . . . you're right, of course. Come on, Tink. We don't want any silly mothers, anyway.

(*They disappear from the window. Again there is a short silence.* WENDY, JOHN *and* MICHAEL *appear at the window and climb through.*)

MICHAEL   I think I have been here before . . .

JOHN   It's your home, idiot!

MICHAEL   Who are the people?

WENDY   Mother and father!

MICHAEL   Then you are not weally our mother, Wendy?

WENDY   Oh, dear! It really is high time we were back.

JOHN   Let's wake mother up and put our hands over her eyes!

WENDY   No, we had better break it gently.

(*They get into bed.*)

WENDY   One, two, three . . .

WENDY
JOHN   }   (*quietly*) Mother!
MICHAEL

(*Nothing happens.*)

WENDY
JOHN   } (*more loudly*) Mother!
MICHAEL

MR DARLING   Wha . . . mumnumn . . .

MRS DARLING   (*sleepily*) I thought I heard voices.

JOHN   You did! It's us, we're back!

MRS DARLING   George, the plumbing's making noises again.

MR DARLING   Nonsense, go to sleep!

MICHAEL   No, weally! Look! We're in bed!

MRS DARLING   There it is again. It could almost be the children. Oh, what I would give to hear their silvery voices again.

WENDY   Silvery voices? These two sound more like donkeys!

MRS DARLING   That sounds just like Wendy!

JOHN   Oh, do look at the bed, you silly woman!

MRS DARLING   John, if I ever hear you use language like that again . . . John! Children!

(*The* CHILDREN *jump out of bed and hug* MR *and* MRS DARLING *in turn.*)

MR DARLING   I don't believe it!

MRS DARLING   You have come back at last! Where have you been?

WENDY   We have been to Never Land, to see Peter Pan, the Lost Boys and the pirates!

(PETER *appears at the window.* WENDY *sees him.*)

WENDY   It's Peter! He's here!

(WENDY *goes to the window and pulls* PETER *in.*)

MR DARLING   Who is this, did you say?

WENDY   This is Peter. He lives in Never Land and he saved me from Captain Hook and his crew!

PETER	Hello, Wendy's mother and father. Let me go, Wendy.
WENDY	Wouldn't you like to ask my parents anything, Peter? About our future?
PETER	No . . .
WENDY	Oh, stay with us, Peter. Mother can adopt you, can't she?
MR DARLING	What!
MRS DARLING	George! Of course we can!
PETER	Would you send me to school?
MRS DARLING	Yes!
PETER	And then to an office?
MR DARLING	I suppose so.
PETER	And soon I should be a man?
MRS DARLING	Very soon.
PETER	I don't want to go to school or to an office. I want to be a boy and to have fun!
WENDY	Then could I stay with you, Peter?
MRS DARLING	Certainly not! Now I've got you home again, I mean to keep you!
PETER	Wendy, do you really want me to stay with you?
WENDY	Of course, but it's up to you.
PETER	Well . . . what do you think, audience? should I stay with Wendy?
AUDIENCE	Yes!
PETER	Louder! I can't hear you. Should I stay?
AUDIENCE	Yes!
PETER	Gosh! I've just seen more bridgework than Brunel! Fair enough, then — I'll stay!

MR DARLING	Over my dead body!
MRS DARLING	George!
MR DARLING	"George" nothing. I'm not having another one to eat us out of house and home!
OMNES	Oh, yes you are!
MR DARLING	Oh, no I'm not!
OMNES	Oh, yes you are!
MR DARLING	Alright, alright! We'll take him in! Might as well take everyone in!
WENDY	Splendid! You can come in now, boys!
MR DARLING	Boys! Plural? What boys?

(*The* LOST BOYS *enter one by one through the window, in ascending size order, followed by* TINK. MR DARLING *sinks lower and lower with each arrival. If desired,* NANA *can burst through the door at this stage, to add yet more confusion to the scene.*)

MR DARLING	By the Lord Harry! What are they? And what is she?
MRS DARLING	Children, dear.
MR DARLING	You had better put down some newspapers, Mary.
WENDY	Can they stay?
MR DARLING	Never! Eleven? Who would have all these children? You would have to be stark staring mad!
MRS DARLING	Children brighten a home, George!
MR DARLING	I know. They never turn the lights off!
MRS DARLING	But, there is so much we could give them.
MR DARLING	I dare say a few good hidings wouldn't go amiss.
MRS DARLING	Oh, please dear. They are all so lovely!
PETER	Even Tink?
TINK	Yes, I am aren't I? And I want to stay, too.

LOST BOYS }   Yes please, George. Let us stay!
TINK

MR DARLING   I know I shall regret this, but yes, you can stay.

OMNES   Hurrah!

MR DARLING   Boys, I must see that you are all of good character. Would you always be brave?

LOST BOYS }   Yes!
TINK   }   No!

MR DARLING   Never betray a friend?

LOST BOYS }   Never!
TINK   }   Always!

MR DARLING   Never run from an enemy?

LOST BOYS }   Never!
TINK   }   Of course!

MR DARLING   Always ignore financial gain?

LOST BOYS }   Yes!
TINK   }   Who me?

MR DARLING   Always respect a lady?

LOST BOYS }   Always!
TINK   }   Never!

MR DARLING   Look up to our hard working politicians?

LOST BOYS }   Yes!
TINK   }   Don't make me laugh!

MR DARLING   Have we nothing in common? Still you can stay. Especially Tinkerbell — I have a feeling we may get on.

MRS DARLING   George!

WENDY   Does this mean we have a happy ending, then?

PETER   Yes, Wendy. I think it does. As they say all good things come to an end and so must this Panto. It's been wonderful performing for you, audience; and we hope you learnt something. After all, this an educational show. When you get home you'll say "well, that taught me a lesson". So, it's decided that I and the Lost Boys will stay here. We'll grow up and become responsible citizens. We'll pay tax, vote, buy insurance and take out mortgages — what a prospect! But don't let us despair. All is not lost. Perhaps the next generation will discover Never Land for themselves, and have their share of adventures. Of course, if that were to happen, they would need a captain Hook and all his bully boys. And a crocodile to put some spice into things. Ah, well. All things must pass . . .

HOOK   (*off*) Not so fast, Pan, not so fast.

(*Enter* HOOK, SMEE, *the* PIRATES *and* CROCODILE.)

You didn't really think you could get rid of us so easily? We are back in business, all together. And the crocodile has signed on as first mate, now that Smee wants to retire in favour of his fairy! So we are ready for the next set of visitors — whenever they arrive. And there's no hurry — after all . . . time is fleeting . . .

(*Reprise of the Time Warp, with as much gusto as possible and audience participation if they feel brave. At the end of the song close curtains and re-open at once for walkdown. The Time Warp music is played while bows are taken. When the whole cast is assembled on stage, one more chorus — then the curtains close. The music fades away as the house lights come up.*)

THE END

PRODUCTION NOTES

Suggested additional items to involve children. These can be selected according to numbers of children, range of abilities and time available.

1. Page 5   After WENDY says "go to sleep", there is silence, then nursery toys stretch and get up. They perform a dance to slow, quiet music or sing a 'sleepy' song, or a combination of both. The characters could be a soldier, a clown, a doll, a teddy bear, a golliwog, etc. At the end of this interlude there is silence again before PETER and TINK appear, the toys having subsided back into their previous positions.

2. Page 13   Short reprise of toys dance or song before the music changes to introduce HOOK.

3. Page 14   The children are extra pirates, over and above the speaking parts, to make up the chorus.

4. Page 16   Children dressed as animals come on quietly, followed by the LOST BOYS (noisily) equipped for hunting. All the animals scatter. The BOYS sing a hunting song (such as Hunting Tigers), the animals join in, but every time the BOYS turn round to hunt, the animals scatter. If the BOYS do make a dive for the kill, they invariably miss. As the song ends, the animals melt away.

5. Page 25   All the children join in the Time Warp, dressed as suns, moons, stars, clocks, signs of the Zodiac, etc.

6. Page 31   Children dressed as mermaids dance a sinuous dance and disappear as PETER and WENDY come on. This is set in half light, as if early morning — mist would be nice!

7. Page 37   Extra pirates again.

8. Page 41   When TINK speaks the verse for the second time, a line of children dressed as flowers come into view, rather than the plant. They sing "Never Smile at A Crocodile". At the end they disappear from view once more — after the third magic verse.

9. Page 43   Extra pirates again — join in choruses.

10. Page 48   Extra pirates again.

11.   Page 50   The 'flowers' can join in the duet, suitably choreo-
                    graphed.

12.   Page 52   The 'animals' dance/sing again before SMEE comes on.
                    They scatter as he appears.

13.   Page 56   Chorus for "Crocodile Rock".

14.   Page 57   Extra pirates again. Alter the dialogue slightly to
                    account for the number of pirates. On page 62, the
                    'extra' pirates go offstage and do not reappear. They
                    shout 'abandon ship' as they go.

15.   Page 65   Children perform the audience participation song with
                    TINK and SMEE, instead of the LOST BOYS.

16.   Page 66   The 'toys' reprise their dance after MRS DARLING'S
                    "good night". At the end they subside into their places
                    as PETER and TINK appear.

17.   Page 72   Extra pirates come back. Toys come to life, everybody
                    on stage for The Time Warp.